HYGGE

Live happily and in harmony, restoring the spirit and the body. Discover how to enjoy life pleasures in the simplicity of the minimalist Danish lifestyle, together with your loved ones.

by Vivian Jensen

© Copyright 2020 by Vivian Jensen
All rights reserved

This book is targeted towards offering essential details about the subject covered. The publication is being provided with the thought that the publisher is not mandated to render an accounting or other qualified services. If recommendations are needed, professional or legal, a practiced person in the profession ought to be engaged.

In no way is it legal to recreate, duplicate, or transfer any part of this document in either electronic means or printed format. Copying of this publication is strictly prohibited, and no storage is allowed unless with written authorization from the publisher. All rights reserved.

The details supplied herein are specified to be honest and constant. Any liability, in regards to inattention or otherwise, by any usage or abuse of any directions, processes, or policies confined within is the sole obligation of the recipient reader. Under no circumstances will any form of legal duty or blame be held against the publisher for any reparation, damages, or financial loss due to the information herein, either directly or indirectly. The author owns all copyrights not held by the publisher.

The information herein is provided for educational purposes exclusively and is universal. The presentation of the information is without contractual agreement or any kind of warranty assurance.

All trademarks inside this book are for clarifying purposes only and are possessed by the owners themselves, not allied with this document.

Disclaimer

All erudition supplied in this book is specified for educational and academic purposes only. The author is not in any way in charge of any outcomes that emerge from using this book. Constructive efforts have been made to render information that is both precise and effective, but the author is not to be held answerable for the accuracy or use/misuse of this information.

Foreword

I would like to thank you for taking the very first step of trusting me and deciding to purchase/read this life-transforming book. Thanks for investing your time and resources in this product.

I can assure you of precise outcomes if you will diligently follow the specific blueprint I lay bare in the information handbook you are currently checking out. It has transformed lives, and I firmly believe it will equally change your own life too.

All the information I provided in this Do It Yourself piece is easy to absorb and practice.

Table of Contents

INTRODUCTION **11**

CHAPTER 1: WHAT HYGGE IS **15**
- The origins of the Danish hygge 15
- The basic principles of Hygge 16
- Hygge in the summer 17
- The golden season of Hygge 17
- Benefits of the Hygge lifestyle 20

CHAPTER 2: CULTIVATE THE HYGGE MINDSET **27**
- Comfort 36
- Pleasure 37
- Gratitude 38
- Awareness 38
- Solidarity 39
- Shelter 40
- Hygge decorating strategies for your home 41

CHAPTER 3: WHY IS HYGGE GOOD? **45**
- *For the body* *45*
- *For the mind* *56*

CHAPTER 4: LIKE HAVING A DANISH DAY **63**

CHAPTER 5: BENEFITS OF WELCOMING HAPPINESS AND WELL-BEING **73**
- Serotonin 75
- More optimism 79
- The benefits of gratitude 89
- Traveling makes you happy 92

CHAPTER 6: SIMPLE WAYS TO PRACTICE HYGGE **95**

CHAPTER 7: HOW TO SPEND A DANISH DAY **105**

GOOD AFTERNOON 107
GOOD EVENING 109
THE TAKEAWAY 112
THE CHECKLIST 114

CHAPTER 8: HYGGE AWAY FROM HOME 117

ADD HYGGE ALL YEAR ROUND 120
BRIDE 123
YOUNG PEOPLE/CHILDREN 123

CHAPTER 9: HYGGE'S IMPACT ON THE INDIVIDUAL, SOCIETY AND THE WORLD 129

CHAPTER 10: THE DANISH METHOD OF EDUCATING CHILDREN FOR HAPPINESS 139

EDUCATING CHILDREN ABOUT HAPPINESS IN SCHOOL AND LIFE 140
LIVE HAPPILY WITH THE GAME 141
CONFIDENCE 142
EMPATHY 143
SINCERITY 143
COURAGE 144

CHAPTER 11: HOW TO APPLY HYGGE REALISTICALLY IF YOU HAVE AN AVOIDABLE LIFESTYLE 147

ADOPT THE LIGHT 148
COMMUNITY 148
SAVOR THE FLAVORS 148
HYGGE AT WORK 149
HYGGE IN THE GYM 149
CREATING HYGGE: IMPLEMENTING THE MOMENT 151
CREATING HYGGE: COMPONENTS FOR A HYGGE DAY 152

CHAPTER 12: IMPROVE PERFORMANCE AND JOB SATISFACTION THROUGH HYGGE 155

- Employee welfare 155
- Physical well-being 156
- Emotional well-being 162
- Spend your lunch break outdoors 163
- Personalize your desk or workstation 164
- Give employees sincere recognition 165
- Collaboration between employees 166

CHAPTER 13: PRACTICAL HYGGE 173

- A personal corner 175
- The ideal temperature 175
- Design and order 176
- A quality bed (also aesthetic) 176
- Hygge style bedroom 177
- Hygge style lounge 177
- Hygge style bathroom 178
- Hygge, the way to "happy" clothing 178
  - *Hygge and me* 179
  - *The Danish palette* 181
- Hygge inspirations for cooking 181

CHAPTER 14: PRACTICAL HYGGE: HOW TO CUSTOMIZE YOUR WARDROBE 189

- The checklist 190

CHAPTER 15: PRACTICAL HYGGE: HUNGRY FOR HYGGE 197

FOCACCIA AND BREAD FOR BREAKFAST 198

- Rugbrød: Danish rye bread 199
- Porridge: staple food 200
- Ebleskivers: Danish pancakes 201

LUNCH AND LIGHTER FARE 202

    TOMATO SOUP, NORDIC STYLE 204

    HOT SMOKED SALMON: SCANDINAVIAN STAPLE 205

CHAPTER 16: PRACTICAL HYGGE: HOLIDAYS AND HYGGE SEASONS 209

    CHRISTMAS IS THE MOST BEAUTIFUL HYGGELIGT TIME OF THE YEAR 212

    SPRING: RENEW AND INVIGORATE 214

    EASTER REDUX 217

    SUMMER: THE OUTDOORS IS OURS 219

    FESTIVAL OF THE DAYS, FROM MEMORIAL TO WORK 221

    AUTUMN: COZY UP 224

    THANKSGIVING ISN'T JUST FOR AMERICANS 226

CHAPTER 17: PRACTICAL HYGGE: PARENTING, RELATIONSHIPS, AND SOLIDARITY 227

    PARTNERS: NURTURING RELATIONSHIPS 231

    FRIENDS: ESTABLISHING BONDS 234

    FAMILY: INTERGENERATIONAL TOGETHERNESS 237

CONCLUSION 239

Introduction

Difficult to explain well and even more difficult to pronounce, the Danish term "Hygge" (pronounced "hugga") has suddenly become popular around the world. It literally translates to "warmth, coziness", but it contains so much more. What does the word Hygge mean? We can say that Hygge is typical Danish like æbleskiver, the typical Christmas pancakes, but it has an even more beneficial effect on the spirit!

In essence, this means creating a welcoming atmosphere and enjoying the beauty of life with loved ones. Candlelight is cleansing. How to get comfortable watching movies with your loved ones. And there's nothing safer than sitting with friends and family and chatting about big and small things in life. Maybe that's why Denmark has some of the happiest people in the world.

In a technical sense, the word "Hygge" comes from a Norwegian word meaning "well-being". As we know it, it first appeared in Danish writings in the 19th century and has since evolved to encompass an entire cultural phenomenon known most prominently in Denmark. This is the technical aspect of his linguistic history, and every Dane you meet will think of every other word in their language before deeming Hygge "technical".

Many people are not interested in the origin of this term as much as in its evolution. How did Hygge evolve into what it is today for Danish culture? How do we implement it in our environment? Does Hygge have a specific color, slogan or mascot? Does it have a lively following or does it have a hint book or user guide? Does it have rules, regulations and expectations? People are more intrigued by the origins of how it came about in practice.

In Denmark, there are many different factors. Their climate is mostly dark and cold, with winter being the longest season of the year, which means Danes spend a lot of time indoors. Hence, their Hygge lifestyle has evolved to implement the things they can enjoy inside. This is where we get the stereotypical images of warm socks, soft candles, a crackling fireplace, and a comfy blanket hanging at the knees. But this is simply a person's version of Hygge given the everyday circumstances.

Hygge makes itself felt in the very being of the person who implements the lifestyle. In American culture, a "lifestyle" comes with certain rules, such as a diet or a new exercise program. There is a "1-2-3" and a "step by step" in the dance of something new, which is why many of us have a hard time understanding what Hygge is. Because it is felt, not defined.

What Americans may lack is the conscious part. In Denmark, Hygge and the idea of carving out these times, is a conscious effort that has taken place throughout their life, which means that less time is spent on bringing work home and more time is spent leaving work for family commitments and friends. Their problem of "defining" it for us and describing its "origins" arises because, for them, that conscious effort has always existed. Just like people make a conscious effort to drive to a bar and grab a cup of anything, Danes make a conscious effort to carve out these slow, intimate moments with the people they care about. If you ask someone to give up that morning coffee run, they might look at you with a stunned expression ... just like asking a Dane to give up his hygge. It's part of their DNA, so to speak.

Chapter 1: What Hygge is

The origins of the Danish hygge

The term Hygge comes from Old Norse, where it had a meaning close to "well-being". It first appeared in a Danish text around the end of the 18th century and has since become part of the language. As you will soon discover on your visit to Denmark, the term Hygge can be applied to anything and the Danes use it for all aspects of daily life.

If you are used to spending time on social networks, especially the "photographic" ones such as Instagram or Pinterest, you have most likely come across the hashtag #hygge, perhaps wondering what it is. Let's say first of all that it is not an acronym, but a Danish word that is used all over the world because it is considered untranslatable. This complicates the explanation of its meaning.

With the term Hygge we want to describe an atmosphere, a particular feeling, what you feel when you feel at home, safe, in total relaxation and well-being. It is described mainly for images, such as that of a cup of tea in front of the fireplace, with a good book and a blanket (the most common).

The basic principles of Hygge

There are some words that represent the Hygge manifesto and they were collected by Meik Wiking, the director of the Copenhagen Happiness Research Institute (Denmark). The keywords are: intimacy, atmosphere, presence (understood as physical and mental presence, which also consists of turning off cell phones to create a deep connection), pleasure (deriving from simple things, like a sweet treat), equality (in conversation and in the division of tasks), gratitude, harmony, comfort, respite (for this reason it is forbidden to discuss politics), sharing (especially through memories and narratives), refuge (choosing a place of peace and safety).

Hygge is an intangible, abstract concept, but it has flavors, smells, sounds, you can see it, touch it and above all you can try it. Like it? Create the right atmosphere. Hygge is considered the fundamental ingredient in the recipe for the pursuit of happiness according to the Danes who are considered one of the happiest peoples in the world, especially thanks to the welfare model of their country, which reduces the risk of uncertainty and anxiety in citizens.

Hygge in the summer

If you visit Denmark in the summer, don't worry - Hygge never goes on vacation! A picnic in the park, a barbecue with friends, outdoor concerts, street parties and bike rides are all very Hygge things, especially when done "Danish".

The golden season of Hygge

The highlight of Hygge is Christmas. Denmark has a fundamentally centuries-old lifestyle, but when the Christmas holidays come, it brings out the best in itself. To fight the long, dark winter, the Danes show off their best weapons: Hygge and millions of candles! If you've been to Denmark before or strolled around Copenhagen around this time, you have an idea of what they can do here with lighting, gløgg (local mulled wine), blankets and maxi scarves. If not, it's time to go and see for yourself! The most welcoming month of the year is December. Hygge time, as the Danes like to call that atmosphere and sense of coziness typical of winter. The desire to be in front of a fireplace in the sweet company of loved ones.

The Oxford Dictionaries Word of the year, "post-truth", entered the final with other terms related to the political news of 2016: "Brexiteer" and "alt-right", for example. But not only that, since there was also "hygge", a Danish word defined "a type of reassuring intimacy and conviviality that generates a feeling of fulfillment or well-being". Hygge does not have a direct translation into other languages: in English what comes closest to it is "cozy", which however has only part of its meaning.

"Associated with relaxation, patience and gratitude, Hygge has long been considered part of the Danish national character," writes the New Yorker, recalling how the term was already in an article published on its pages in 1957, according to author Robert Shaplen, " omnipresent ":" The sidewalks are full of smiling, hyggeligt people who keep taking their hats off between them and looking at a stranger with an expression that indicates they would like to know him well enough to take it off in front of him too."

Winter, of course, is the triumph of Hygge, with its candles, slippers, wool sweater, wood, milk and chocolate mugs and fireplace, an emblem of the Danish word concept, which it can be used as a noun, as an adjective, as a verb and even in a compound word: Hygge bukser, for example, is that pair of old pants that you would never wear to go out, but at home they are prodigiously comfortable. Hygge, the New Yorker specifies, is found in a bakery or in the heat of a sauna during the winter, and its prevalence in Denmark is such that doctors recommend "tea and Hygge" for those with seasonal flu.

Incidentally, the Scandinavian term has also turned into a fairly successful editorial trend: "at least six books" on Hygge were published last year in the United States, and more will arrive next year. And in Britain the concept was so successful that it led Charlotte Higgins to dedicate an investigation to the Guardian.

Denmark is therefore spreading a culture that is functional to the enhancement of its image and tourism. He understood what his uniqueness is. He understood people's needs. Denmark has infused the warmth of a cup of hot chocolate into a trend that defines its precise identity. The true art of Hygge is a feeling of well-being: the deep pleasure of relaxing with friends, enjoying good food and creating an atmosphere of warmth and intimacy.

The Danes have made it a real brand, which pushes tourists to visit the region of Northern Europe in the coldest months of the year, with the desire to live a unique experience, made of hospitality, simplicity and a return to small joys. Hygge is a true art, a culture, a way of life. And the tradition for which they were proclaimed, in 2016, the happiest country in the world. In a few months this brand went viral, creating a real trend. Hygge is easy to understand and desire, as an emotion and as an experience.

Benefits of the Hygge lifestyle

There are many different benefits to leading the kind of lifestyle that Hygge offers. For many, the key is to reduce stress and all related health complications. For others, however, it has very different impacts that have other medical benefits as well.

The Nordic region lifestyle includes an enhanced segment of Hygge that comes from being outside. This allows them to admire the natural beauty that surrounds them, get away from their electronic devices and unplug, and naturally encourages the body to move and thrive in the environment around them. Medically, this means healthier routines have a greater chance of being ingrained. Many studies have shown that exercise outdoors, even with just a stroll, entails more benefits than working out in the gym.

Hunting is another popular pastime in this culture, so being in nature is synonymous with clearing your minds and leaving your worries behind. If sweating in nature doesn't seem relaxing, being in the middle of it with no noise or worry while breathing is also considered a Hygge-type moment. Air is cooler than the air inside your home, and although it can be filtered better, pollution air in most homes is higher than outside. This means that "getting fresh air" can stimulate the brain in ways that you can't stay inside.

Another huge benefit of Hygge is what happens when stress levels in the body drop. Cortisol is the chemical usually associated with stress, but it has a wider impact than that. It is a vital chemical that secretes from the adrenal gland and moderates a multitude of them bodily functions. Blood sugar levels, metabolism, blood pressure and immune responses are just some of the vital components of our body that Cortisol directly affects. Cortisol naturally fluctuates as our body needs it, regulating everything from constricting blood vessels to leveling blood sugars. With a hectic lifestyle, the body doesn't have a chance to return to a "normal state" before Cortisol has to step in and regulate something back to normal.

This can lead to some medical problems, which can worsen if the adrenal glands become fatigued because they can no longer keep up with the production of Cortisol needed to regulate the body's systems. This can result in sleep disturbances, decreased bone density, blood sugar imbalances, and even decreased muscle mass. Not only that, but Cortisol sticks to abdominal fats, fixing them in their positions, and this also leads to a number of other medical problems.

From a biological standpoint, then, Hygge is simply a time when stress reduction and stressful external influences are negated. This allows the body to lower Cortisol levels, which allows the body to return to normal. If Hygge is consistently indulged, the body has a chance to heal from some of the internal damage Cortisol tends to do, such as muscle wear and damage to the gastrointestinal tract.

Only these two benefits alone increase the happiness someone experiences because the chemical reactions within the brain are not intruded by a constant rise in Cortisol.

While there is a lot of emphasis on what's "natural" in Danish Hygge culture interpretation, the simple fact is that the biggest advantage of this lifestyle is its lack of rules. It's all based on how you feel internally at any given time, and as long as the individual is disconnected from the electronics, puts away work and finds ways to relax and release stress, the lifestyle can be adapted to any person. Some may find their Hygge moments in a club by dancing in a crowd, while someone who likes to be alone can sit at home and read a good book. Both are Hygge moments within wildly separate worlds simply based on how the person feels.

The Hygge lifestyle and what it promotes may also ward off some mental disease. People struggling with seasonal depression, drastic mood swings, and feelings of anxiety have reported that making Hygge their new way of life helps them regulate symptoms on their own. Many have talked about reducing drug dosages and some have talked about stopping altogether. It promotes a better lifestyle when it comes to individual health and focuses on being kinder to yourself. This can eliminate unnecessary feelings of guilt that can cause anxiety episodes, which can help turn off an individual's negative thought coil.

A key fact of Hygge is the absence of stress, but if you find yourself in a stressful situation and can't get rid of it, Hygge can then be used to deal with stress. For example, you are already 10 minutes late for your workday, but you know you can't give up that morning cup of coffee if you expect to be useful. So when you go to your favorite bar, a Hygge move could spend an extra $ 1.00 to get a bigger size and add your favorite flavor. So, sipping on the flavor you like can help relieve the stress that's already running through your system.

The benefits of a Hygge lifestyle aren't simply emotional; they are doctors. Adopting the lifestyle that Danes regard as a natural lifestyle has revolutionized the lives of thousands of people, and it's all because they have decided to live outside the norm of their own culture. However, many interested people are still not entirely sure how to apply Hygge to their life.

And for this there is an answer.

Chapter 2: Cultivate the Hygge mindset

Unfortunately, many people will start calling candles Hygge, thus starting the cycle of turning a lifestyle into an advertising campaign. This is exactly what happened to the Hygge lore. While Hygge took on a unique form in Western culture, becoming something very similar to Hygge, it was usurped by consumerism. Now when you talk about Hygge, the first thing another person will think of is Zen candles, Zen water fountains, or even Zen tea. In other words, rather than imagining the basic feeling and mindset of Zen, the average person will imagine the product line being sold at the local supermarket. You can certainly create a Zen ambiance or even a Zen mindset by lighting candles, listening to a water fountain, and even drinking hot tea. However, you can also create a Zen mindset by taking a walk in nature, spending time with a cat or dog, or even listening to relaxing music. Unfortunately, the items used to reach the Hygge objectives have been exchanged for the objective itself. Anyone who is truly interested in Zen and achieving a Zen mindset will steer clear of the objects that the name "Zen" is associated with, as they know this is nothing more than a marketing gimmick. Fortunately, enough people are aware of the problem and are striving to return the true meaning of Zen to its name.

While some may see Hygge as a sentiment, philosophy, or even a passing fad, the fact is that Hygge is a perspective. It is a way of seeing all of life, from daily activities to the hopes and dreams that define life. Every aspect of life will take on a Hygge perspective when you start living a Hygge lifestyle. Understanding the true nature of Hygge is crucial for anyone who wants to incorporate it into their lifestyle. Without this understanding, Hygge can follow the path of countless other cultural traditions and movements such as hippies, bohemians, hipsters and even Zen. All of these traditions started as a lifestyle revolution, promoting a different approach to life, love and happiness. They all made an impact for a while, influencing the way people lived in many ways. Unfortunately, over time, the true nature of these movements was lost in the advertising campaign, which replaced the hippie view of life with hippie-style jeans, blouses and even incense. Likewise, the lifestyle of the Bohemian movement has become little more than a fashion trend with some musical genres incorporating the name. This cycle of events is seemingly inevitable as the overwhelming culture of materialism always seems to corrupt, co-opt and assimilate any other culture or lifestyle it comes into contact with. No matter how powerful a movement is when it begins, it eventually succumbs to the unstoppable influences of the consumer culture around it.

One way to keep the true nature of Hygge as a perspective alive and well is to constantly distance the concept of Hygge from the things that help manifest it. A perfect example of this is the use of candles to create a Hygge ambiance. While it's true that candles and the light they provide can create a Hygge feeling in any room, referring to candles themselves as Hygge is missing the point. Candles are candles, nothing more and nothing less.

Hygge faces the same challenge in Western culture. Before long, candles will be given the nickname "Hygge", as will blankets, slippers, mugs and even varieties of hot chocolate. It will probably be only a few more Christmases before you can purchase a Hygge gift set, complete with all these things in an "authentic" Danish gift basket. It is imperative, therefore, that anyone engaging in the practice of Hygge retains the true meaning of the concept. Never allow yourself to buy things just because they are attributed to the Hygge lifestyle. As previously mentioned, Hygge can mean something different to each person who practices it. Certainly, candles help establish the Hygge because they allow you to turn off the electric lights and unplug from modern technology.

The most important thing is to determine what Hygge means to you and to decide what elements are needed to establish it in your heart and mind. After all, this is the whole point of Hygge: it is the process of creating a very specific state of mind. This mood can be defined as welcoming, joyful, peaceful, or any other word that best describes what Hygge means to you. Just as Hygge can mean many different things, so it can take many different things to manifest it. Therefore, don't get too involved with the "tools of the trade". Instead, keep your mind focused on the feeling of Hygge and the impact this feeling has on your life.

There is another very important aspect of Hygge that can only be understood when Hygge is seen as a perspective. This aspect is that the Hygge comes from within, not from without. As such, the key isn't trying to find something that possesses Hygge to create the Hygge experience. Instead, the trick is to find things that inspire the Hygge that already exists in your heart and mind. As a state of mind, Hygge is something that must be aroused, not ingested. This is why people can find Hygge in a wide variety of objects and experiences. Objects and experiences do not contain Hygge; rather the individual who uses them possesses a Hygge mood. Next, take Hygge with you wherever you go and whatever you do.

Instead of trying to use the things traditionally associated with Hygge, start exploring all the things that resonate with the Hygge that resides within you. You might be surprised at the things that can inspire a Hygge response. They can be things associated with your childhood, or they can be things associated with your favorite color, scent, or flavor. Sure, hot chocolate is commonly referred to as an integral part of Hygge, but if chocolate isn't your favorite flavor, you may find something else that works best for you. You don't have to try to simply follow what others are doing, as this is another avenue for turning a lifestyle into a stencil trend. Instead, use what others do as a point of inspiration. Start with hot chocolate, for example, but switch to other hot drinks you might like, such as tea, milk, or even hot mocha. Just remember that the object itself is simply the tool, not the goal or the result.

Another thing to consider is the fact that Hygge is not a fixed point in time. Just because something inspires Hygge one day doesn't mean it will have the same effect another day. Consequently, it is important to discover various things that inspire Hygge so that you can switch between them, as your mood requires. A perfect example of this is reading. Many will argue that reading is an activity that exudes Hygge, and this can be true for many reasons. However, there may be a time when your eyes are tired or your body doesn't feel like sitting for a long time. In these cases, reading, no matter how Hygge may be, may not be what you need to do. Instead, a walk in the woods, a bike ride or any other physical activity could meet the needs of your body at that time. Alternatively, if your eyes need rest, then simply listening to some soothing music while relaxing with your eyes closed might do the trick. As your mood and energy levels change from day to day, it's important to stay flexible with your Hygge practices. By recognizing that Hygge comes from within, you'll be able to be less dependent on specific activities to feed your Hygge mood. This will allow you to choose from a wide variety of things, which means that you can access different tools to suit your different moods and energy levels. You will be able to depend less on specific activities to feed your Hygge mood.

This approach can also take on a seasonal connotation, especially in countries that have a wider range of seasonal climates than Denmark. In the United States, where it can get extremely cold in the winter, but also extremely hot and sunny in the summer, tapping into different sources of Hygge can be extremely beneficial. Sitting by the fire might be just the thing in the dead of winter, lounging on a beach, listening to the sounds of the ocean, and feeling the gentle summer breeze might do the trick in the dead of summer. Uncovering your various Hygge faces will help you keep a Hygge mood all year round, regardless of the season or weather conditions. Again, you need to remember that your Hygge is inside, waiting to be "turned on" from external stimuli. This will help you avoid getting stuck in a rut with certain Hygge activities. Sure, the fireplaces and hot chocolate are great, but you shouldn't rely on them in July in Florida!

Therefore, by finding what inspires your Hygge in every likely scenario and environment, you can rest assured that your Hygge will always be close at hand. Finding Hygge inspiration in many things also means that you won't have to pack an extra suitcase just to carry your Hygge items with you when you travel. The less you depend on specific things, the more likely you are to be able to experience Hygge no matter where you are. This applies to both business trips and vacations. If you have to travel for business, you need to find numerous and easy ways to feed your Hygge mind. It won't be that hard to do, however, as long as you cling to the idea of taking your Hygge with you no matter where you go.

While it's true that you shouldn't get involved with specific objects or activities to keep your mind Hygge, it's also true that when you find something that works, you should use it completely. If you fall in love with a particular piece of clothing, like a sweatshirt, and it fills you with Hygge every time you wear it, wear it as often as possible. Don't be afraid of what others might think or say. Wear your sweatshirt every day if you want. In the case of summer dresses, maybe you have a favorite pair of sandals or a favorite tee that arouses your inner Hygge every time you wear it. Again, don't be afraid to consume them. Use it while it works but know that when it stops working you can find other things to take its place.

Another example of objects of inspiration can be found in music. Sometimes you'll come across a song that completely resonates, bringing your Hygge levels to overflowing. You may be tempted to play the song over and over, listening to the music and lyrics until you feel like you can explode with the Hygge you hear. Eventually, you may run out of the song or find something else to take its place; however, as long as it works, you should listen to it as often as possible. The important thing is to keep your Hygge alive and well at all times. Therefore, whenever you discover something that achieves that goal, make the most of it, no matter how boring or annoying it may be for some people around you!

How does Hygge help happiness?

Hygge is a Scandinavian way of life that promotes calm and warmth. It celebrates joy and health and can be achieved in several ways besides just decorating. Here are some methods you can integrate Hygge into your life:

- ➢ Surround yourself with family and friends;
- ➢ Love easy pleasures;
- ➢ Be joyful and present;
- ➢ Stay an hour in excess;
- ➢ Barbeque outside;
- ➢ Reuse and recycle;
- ➢ Request;
- ➢ Don't stress;
- ➢ Enjoy your environment;
- ➢ I love a great book;
- ➢ Hygge principles;
- ➢ Atmosphere.

Having a Hygge home makes everything easier and it doesn't take long to create a Hygge vibe. Light a few candles and you're halfway there! Candles are essential for your Hygge moment. If you have a fireplace, this is a huge plus. If not, get creative with your lighting. Rather than using bright lights that illuminate the entire room, consider producing delicate islands of light that welcome an individual to curl up with a great book or any knitting.

Another way to make your home more Hygge would be to invite nature into your home. Decorate your home with flowers and plants or develop a herb garden on your kitchen window sill. Instead, if you're a black-thumbed plant killer like me, you can go outdoors with family and friends. A trip to nature gives a feeling of relaxation and can help put things in perspective.

Comfort

Hygge frees you to feel relaxed and at ease. This usually means no makeup and losing clothes, like worn yoga leggings you can't bear to part with. A sofa that relaxes you with comfortable cushions is Hygge. So it's a delicate blanket and your hair pulled back into a loose bun.

Go out? It's just as Hygge to cover up using a vest, lace socks and a comfy sweater that threatens to wear you out completely. Consider wearing clothes that make you feel good and comfortable. This does not mean giving up on fashion; however, it will mean finding clothes that are both trendy and easy to wear.

Pleasure

Hygge encourages you to find life's basic pleasures, which can often be right there in front of you for your shoot if you have the right attitude. The food is hugely satisfying and therefore a huge part of Hygge. However, it's not just about the pleasure that comes from eating. Consider how the food arrives on your table. There is pleasure in gardening, canning or making your watches.

Hygge allows you to let your obligations take a temporary place in the background so that you can be found at the moment and enjoy the great things here and today. Savor your main dish and your dessert. Play with your children. Watch a movie with your significant other. Hold hands and take a walk outside in the park. Take your time to cook and then eat the meal you created. Take some time out and remember the real reasons for your hard work and lifestyle.

Gratitude

In the beginning, many of us are taught to set goals and reach for the stars. It can give you power, but it's easy to get trapped in living solely for your future and forget about enjoying the present. It is important not to forget to be thankful for the life you are currently living, not just for the future. That's where gratitude comes from.

Take a few minutes each day to think about the big things in your life. Let yourself feel how grateful you are for all those items that bring you joy. If someone did something nice for you that made you feel happier and lift your mood, let them know. People experience Hygge feelings of bliss and joy by assuming a joyful and grateful attitude.

Awareness

When was the last time you stopped and paused for a minute with all your senses? For example, you are in a bar with your best friend. Can you hear the cry of the espresso machine in the hum of people talking? Did your windows cook? Would you smell freshly made java? Does tea warm your hands? Would you taste the honey you pumped inside?

Maybe you are camping with your loved ones and enjoying a day around the fire. Are you currently listening to the fire pit? Can you smell the burnt wood mixed with the aroma of pines and earth? Are you seeing the faces of your loved ones glow in the light of the flames? Can you taste the flavors of roasted and melted marshmallows as they land on your tongue? Is it true that firefights away from the freezing air and warms you from the inside out?

The longer you open to the senses of joy in the present moment, the more Hygge it will become for you. It takes awareness to get there, which takes work and dedication to gratitude; however, it is a habit worth developing.

Solidarity

When you consider the happiest moments in your daily life, they are usually related to the people you adore. A happier life can be forged by building bonds with other individuals. Take the heart. Hygge isn't about how many friends you have or how big your family is; it's about the quality of the time you spend together. It is possible to have Hygge feelings with a single close friend or a small group of relatives.

Your night could be a game night or even a time for Netflix and chill. It could be a day spent eating and cooking together. You could make something or cook with a close friend. Whatever you are doing, your phone should be turned off and you should give your loved ones your full attention. Hygge encourages people to create lasting and deep bonds according to shared memories.

A few words of warning for you: a hyggeligt gathering is warm and comfortable as it depends on equality and stability in the area. This usually means that everyone is participating in the work involved and everyone has a role to play in any conversation. There are no celebrities and no single individual of more value or importance than another. Furthermore, it usually means that conflicts or even contradictory remarks are not welcome in such a place. There is a time and place to address politics, faith, and other contentious and controversial topics, but if you want a hyggeligt party, avoid such problems and stick to safer areas that will provide a lighthearted and enjoyable conversation.

Shelter

A moment is simply hyggeligt if you are free to open up and reveal that you are truly yourself. Finding a place where you feel safe, with people where you feel safe, is essential for Hygge. Inside this place, you shouldn't hesitate to wear old or worn-out clothes, don't wear makeup and be who you really are, as your friends and family won't judge you because they love the person you are. As Meik Wiking described it in his novel "Hygge's Little Book", these individuals are "your tribe" and these encounters take place in your "area of peace and security".

Hygge decorating strategies for your home

Hygge is related to creating a safe and sheltered space for family members. Plus, coupled with a period of family social events just around the corner, it's the perfect time to Hygge your home! When decorating, it is vital to keep things simple to fully immerse yourself in this joyful and comfortable lifestyle.

1. **Stick to a neutral decorating plan**

The plan for your home's stylistic theme should never be too overbearing, as far as Hygge is concerned. Anything you use to enhance your Hygge home should add to a climate of accommodation and stability. Following non-partisan shading palettes is more important when creating a soothing space, and using muted colors like light grays, tans and creams can create a pleasant area for you and your guests.

2. **Create a pleasant atmosphere**

Comfort is key to the Hygge style. I approach this by integrating almost all furniture with upholstery and upholstered sofas. Curl up on the love seat with layers of pillows and blankets to relax in a warm place. You can also do this by creating comfortable alcoves, such as a window seat or love seat. All of this makes for a great place to unwind with a good book and a cup of hot chocolate for a few moments of stability and calm.

3. **Enhance your area with candles**

When you consider candles, what is the first thing that comes to your mind? Maybe it's a relaxing bath before a quiet night with a book. These activities are included in the Hygge lifestyle. The soft, flickering glow of a candle cannot be replicated by anything else and should be used properly throughout the home to create a warm glow.

4. **Illuminate the area with twinkling lights**

Twinkly lights are also great for Hygge design. Together with the simple fact, they are lively and sparkling, they look stunning and magical when hung in your home. You can use them in personal rooms, in the living room or even on your lawn! Like candles, they give off a milder glow and add a nice touch to your home plan without being too overwhelming.

5. Create a flame

Resting around the fire, whether it's outdoors or indoors, is an important part of Hygge culture. It's the perfect time to get together with your loved ones and loved ones and be in charge of the business you run. In this way, the purchase of a fireplace is a fundamental element of the Hygge stylistic design. It speaks to warmth and stability and is more enjoyable when having fun with friends and loved ones.

6. Create a spa-style bathroom

Rather than simply using your bathroom to take a quick shower before the day starts, make it a relaxing getaway to the top. Your bathroom should be a place you visit to rest and recover. To create a wonderful, quiet bathroom, make sure you have plenty of additional hidden storage in drawers and cabinets to provide strategic space for any unwanted clutter. For added happiness, light candles and buy comfortable clothes for a relaxed and peaceful experience.

Chapter 3: Why is Hygge good?

Numerous studies conducted on the level of happiness exhibited by the Danish people have shown that they owe much of it to the practice of Hygge. The attribution of joy, warmth and comfort to this type of lifestyle has led many people to believe that it would also change their life.

But how exactly is this?

While probably the best-known benefit of a hyggeligt lifestyle is to enjoy the simple pleasures of life with loved ones, there are many other benefits you might expect by taking the initiative to apply its principles to various aspects of your day in everyday life.

For the body

Hygge promotes feelings of security and calm. If sustained for a reasonable period, this type of environment allows the body to adapt accordingly. Rather than always being ready for times of stress and danger, the body would be able to relax and focus its resources on other functions, such as healing, self-cleaning, and fighting bacteria and viruses.

Once you reach this bodily state, you will be able to reap the following physical benefits of Hygge:

1. **Lower levels of the stress hormone**

The human body is wired to react accordingly to various types of danger. In ancient times, this mechanism allowed humanity to survive against predators and the dangerous forces of danger. These threats have not completely disappeared over time, but rather have evolved in ways that significantly affect daily life.

For example, everyone faces the hassle of meeting the demands of different aspects of life - taking care of the family, dealing with a heavy workload or looming bill deadlines. Although these stressors are quite different from repelling wild beasts, the body recognizes them as threats to its own life.

When this happens, the body releases Cortisol, the main stress hormone, and adrenaline into the bloodstream. This would then result in:

- High heart rate;
- Increased blood pressure;
- A higher blood glucose level;
- Impaired immune system;

> Digestive system, reproductive system and cell growth suppressed.

These changes in the body allow a person to have more energy for movement and brain function. More bodily resources are also allocated for cell and tissue repair. Ultimately, stress hormones promote functions that might help in a fight or flight situation and repress those that don't contribute much or not at all.

Once the stressor has been eliminated or minimized, the effects of Cortisol and adrenaline also dissipate until the body is restored to its normal functioning. However, many people can't get rid of stress long enough to allow for cooling.

Prolonged exposure to stress hormones tends to be highly disruptive to nearly all important bodily functions. As such, it would put anyone at serious risk of developing:

> Various cardiovascular diseases;

> Weight gain;

> Mental disabilities;

> Digestive problems;

> Inability to sleep;

> Depression;

> Anxiety;

> Severe headaches.

Given these likely effects of overexposure to stress hormones, it is important to learn how to cope with stressors healthily.

Practicing Hygge is considered to be one of the most effective ways to do this. This type of lifestyle promotes the idea of removing yourself from situations that could be emotionally overwhelming and instead, focus on the things that could make you happy.

These principles are easy enough to apply than you might think. Compared to other lifestyle trends, Hygge doesn't require a lot of effort or money. The less you spend, the more hyggeligt your life would be. Examples of hyggeligt moments that could significantly reduce the number of stress hormones include but are not limited to:

> Sitting by a fireplace;

> Bake cookies, cakes and other types of pastries;

> Have an intimate dinner with family and friends;

> Curl up under a thick blanket with your loved one;

> Wear a cozy cardigan;

> Go for a hike in nature.

Essentially, Hygge means being kind to yourself, the people around you, and the environment. Appreciating the simple pleasures in life is a good way to give your body enough time to recover from the effects of stress hormones.

2. **Better sleep quality**

Sleep plays an important role in achieving good physical, mental and emotional well-being. During this time, the body may rest and repair itself. Growth and development are also given a boost, especially among children.

The right amount of sleep varies by age group, but on average seven hours of sleep could do wonders for the body. Failure to achieve the prescribed amount could lead to sleep deprivation, which in turn affects:

- Vulnerability to diseases, such as heart disease, stroke, high blood pressure and diabetes;
- Memory and concentration;
- Control of mood and emotions;
- Performance when awake;
- Personal safety.

Getting the correct number is critical, but insufficient if you have achieved it by artificial means, such as taking sleeping pills, or if you have woken up feeling tired after a restless sleep. The quality of your sleep is just as important as the number of hours you slept.

Health experts recommend different strategies for getting sufficient quality sleep. For example:

- o Establish and follow a ritual before going to bed;
- o Maintain the same sleep schedule every day, regardless of whether it's a weekday or weekends;
- o Refrain from using any electronic device at least one hour before bedtime.

These strategies have proven effective for many people. Hygge, however, increases the expected result from taking any or all of these initiatives. It can also make it easier for you to create a lasting habit from these sleep-inducing behaviors.

Applying Hygge to the way you sleep is pretty simple to do. For many, it starts by turning the bedroom into a relaxing sleep sanctuary. Anything that can make both your body and mind feel at rest can be placed somewhere in this space: fluffy pillows, knitted blankets or scented candles. Having these items in the bedroom could help trigger the regular release of serotonin, the main hormone linked to a restful night.

Once the ideal setting is reached, hyggeligt practices could be part of your normal sleep ritual to further relax the body and mind. Here are some of the highly recommended activities you should consider:

- Take a nice long hot bath;
- Listening to relaxing music;
- Performing meditation or mindfulness exercises;
- Write down the things you are thankful for in a daily journal.

Keep in mind, however, that Hygge doesn't give a full guarantee that it will fix any sleep problems you have, such as insomnia or sleep paralysis. At best, it could help you create an environment that would increase your chances of achieving the ideal sleep duration and quality for you. For more severe and persistent sleep-related problems, you should seek the advice of an experienced doctor.

3. **Better weight management**

Hygge is not a diet plan nor a weight loss measure. What it does for weight control is to improve the way you eat, sleep and have fun. It wouldn't make you lose ten pounds right away, but practicing Hygge will help keep your body in good shape.

4. **Be aware of what you eat and drink**

Taking the time to savor and enjoy every bite and sip will help you regulate your eating habits. Instead of settling for frozen meals and fast food, which both contain high levels of sodium and trans fat, you'd be more aware of the things you consume every day.

Also, chewing food slowly would lengthen the time to eat. According to experts, doing so would make you feel full even if you haven't eaten a significant amount of food yet.

5. **Turn the act of eating into a special occasion**

Due to the many demands of modern life, some people may be tempted to eat a quick meal in front of the TV rather than cooking and sharing meals with the people you care about.

Hygge promotes special social experiences for everyone involved. It's not just about eating good food. It also encourages the use of good music, an engaging atmosphere, and pleasant conversations with the people who eat with you. This way, you will be able to more easily switch to a healthier diet that could fill both your belly and heart.

6. Making your favorite food rewards for good performance and results

Completely depriving yourself of special treats, such as chocolate truffles or special types of cheese, could be counterproductive when it comes to weight control. Preventing yourself from eating certain foods would increase your desire for it, which leads to overeating.

Indulging yourself occasionally and in moderation is extremely hyggeligt. Eating your favorite food is an enjoyable experience that could end a particularly busy but productive day in a pleasant way.

7. Exercise the body outdoors

A study of more than 800 adults by the Peninsula College of Medicine and Dentistry concluded that there is a significant correlation between outdoor exercise and energy levels. The more they train outdoors, the more they feel revitalized afterward.

Getting an extra boost of energy after a workout would help maintain a regular workout routine. The returns outweigh your efforts, thus inspiring you to do more.

8. Get the right amount of high-quality sleep every day

Sleep deprivation has been linked to obesity mainly due to the hormonal imbalance it causes. Adopting a hyggeligt lifestyle could prevent you from suffering from this condition as it advises various ways on how to achieve good sleep conditions.

But doing it from time to time is not enough. You need to develop and maintain good sleep habits to better manage your weight.

9. **Get away from extremely stressful situations**

One of the many effects of stress hormones on the body is the suppression of the digestive system. If you haven't eaten yet, it would end up spoiling your appetite. On the other hand, if you have already eaten, it could cause digestive problems as it would prevent proper digestion.

Stress could also contribute to weight gain if one of your favorite coping mechanisms is eating food and/or drinking large amounts of alcohol. Associating stressful situations with the temporary relief that food or alcohol might provide can lead to numerous consequences for your overall well-being.

10. **Reduction of vulnerability to serious diseases and infections**

Because Hygge promotes the practice of relaxing your body and mind, getting enough sleep and eating good food in the company of those you care about, it ultimately protects you from various kinds of diseases and illnesses that plague modern humans, such as:

- Different forms of cancer;

- Cardiovascular disease;
- Neurodegenerative diseases;
- Type 1 and type 2 diabetes;
- Kidney related problems.

Don't think Hygge would cure you of these health problems though. It would help you prevent the onset of these diseases and illnesses because studies show that stress, poor nutrition, and a lack of exercise and sleep could lead to disastrous health consequences.

Hygge places great value on these things in life, so applying her principles to all aspects of life could significantly reduce your chances of developing serious health problems now and later.

For the mind

Studies show that creating and maintaining a Hygge environment can help you achieve peace of mind and emotional stability. You would reduce your suffering from anxiety. You would be safe from the constant bombardment caused by your fears and insecurities.

By protecting your mind through the practice of Hygge, you may experience the following mental benefits:

1. Less likely to get depressed

Hygge fights the onset of depression, especially the one that originates from cold and bleak winters: seasonal affective disorder. Just like other forms of depression, SAD makes the affected person feel a drop in mood and energy levels. It could also exacerbate existing depressive tendencies, thus severely affecting one's daily activities.

Although Hygge cannot eliminate depression, it is very effective in reducing a person's vulnerability to this mood disorder. By encouraging people to seek comfort, warmth, and other people, Hygge could minimize the effects of life's harsh realities on your life.

There is no shortage of ways to start adopting Hygge as a lifestyle. The only rule that seems to be to pursue what would make you feel happy and welcoming. Several people respect this by performing these hyggeligt activities:

- o Light scented candles;
- o Cook and enjoy your favorite dish;
- o Spend the evening in front of the fireplace with loved ones;

- Take a long hot shower in the morning;
- Dress up in the most comfortable clothing you can find;
- Read a book while drinking a cup of hot chocolate;
- Admire the landscape as you deliberately inhale and exhale;
- Watch your favorite movie while snuggling under a wool duvet;
- Put your cell phone down and socialize with other people personally.

While many people find these measures effective in reducing their chances of developing depression, that doesn't mean it would work for you too. However, there is no significant harm in trying something that could potentially relieve you of suffering. Just remember to seek professional help when you notice that living Hygge isn't enough to fight your depressive tendencies.

2. Prevents excessive anxiety attacks

Anxiety can be particularly intrusive in everyday life. It affects happiness, well-being, job performance and relationships with other people. Anxiety, in itself, is a natural response of the body and mind to danger and risk, however, it becomes a mental disorder when the worry and fear you feel become too many and too persistent to handle.

To understand if the level of anxiety you are experiencing is worrying for your mental health, here are the common signs and symptoms of anxiety disorder:

- o Breathe in and out at a rapid pace;
- o Feeling tense, restless or nervous frequently or for long periods;
- o Excessive sweating in different parts of the body, such as the forehead, neck, back, armpits or palms of the hand;
- o Problems with appetite and digestion;
- o Believing that a danger or disaster is waiting to happen, even when there is no evidence to be had;
- o Difficulty focusing on current business due to concerns, doubts, or fears about other matters;
- o Inability to fall asleep or stay asleep all night;
- o Deliberately avoiding seeing or doing things you might think will make you feel anxious.

Although mental health professionals can provide treatments and prescriptions to those who suffer from it, studies show that supplementing medications with therapy and support from the people around you produces better long-term results.

Hygge promotes togetherness, not only for entertainment purposes but also to seek the support of others in times of need. When you feel overwhelmed by your worries, doubts, and insecurities, reaching out to someone you trust for help and understanding can prevent you from turning into an even worse state. Showing others that you show them your vulnerable side inspires confidence, which ultimately results in stronger bonds with them.

Knowing that you have someone who supports you can do wonders for your mental and emotional stability. Build close relationships with the people around you by continuously practicing Hygge in every aspect of your life.

3. Greater self-compassion

If you think about it, Hygge wants you to be kind to yourself, even if it encourages you to spend quality time with the people you care about. This rings true, especially when you consider the belief that it is difficult, if not impossible, to take care of others and our surroundings when we are not also concerned about our well-being.

Based on this, you can say that you will begin to feel the effects of the Hygge starting from within. The deliberate things you do to become happier, cozier, and more confident would eventually turn into something you naturally do for yourself.

Turning kindness inward before extending it to others is a sign of a truly hyggeligt lifestyle. Instead of stressing yourself to the point of exhaustion, you can appreciate the value of taking a well-deserved break whenever you need it.

A greater sense of awareness

Being aware means having total awareness of your thoughts, feelings or experiences as they occur. Given such a definition, it is easy to see how the practice of Hygge promotes awareness among its followers.

By focusing on the present, you will be able to appreciate the things that are happening to you, reducing the negative effects of bad memories and worries about the future on your body and mind. Many people equate it with meditation, but there is a fine line between the two. Meditation doesn't require you to stay in the present, but awareness does. In this regard, Hygge seems to be more connected to awareness than to meditation itself.

It offers more opportunities to practice gratitude

In between all that needs to be done throughout the day, it can be easy to forget that you are grateful for the big and small things that make you feel happy, welcoming, and safe. Many people also take for granted the things people do for them, deliberately or not.

Chapter 4: Like having a Danish day

There is an old saying that "The best things in life are free". Hygge promotes this belief because you don't have to buy expensive things or stockpile a lot of things just to feel happiness and comfort.

Hygge living experts know that Hygge is anything but luxury. It is quite humble and low key as it encourages simplicity to opulence and atmosphere to intensity. There's nothing rich about swaddling yourself with a fleece blanket or savoring a cup of hot lemon tea, but both of those things are extremely hyggeligt.

Here are ten great tips that show how Hygge practice can lead to a frugal life:

1. Have fun with the whole group by playing board games

Compared to popular digital forms of entertainment, such as mobile games and streaming apps, board games are considered more hyggeligt. When you play a game on your phone, regardless of whether it is a social game or not, the time you can devote to personal interaction with other people will be greatly reduced.

Instead of being in front of a screen, board games can be just as fun by keeping things Hygge for you and your mates. Variety would probably not be an issue as there is a wide range of board games available nowadays.

In addition to the intimate touch that board games can provide, they can also elicit nostalgic feelings for simpler, slower times. Hours can go by without anyone noticing as everyone is having fun.

2. Throw a party in the pantry with your family and friends

A pantry party is an affordable and innovative way to have fun with your loved ones. The rules are also quite easy to follow.

a. Each participant must bring with them the ingredients of something that can be stored in a pantry or refrigerator, such as chicken broth, vegetable soup, fruit jams, sauces or even dough.

b. Each participant must also bring their containers which would be adequate and sufficient for the objects that will be prepared.

c. Participants will prepare, cook and pack together with the aforementioned pantry items.

d. Divide the finished products among the participants.

At the end of this activity, you wouldn't just have a batch of the merchandise you prepared yourself. You would end up with many homemade pantry items that you would normally have to make yourself or buy from the store. As such, you would save not only money but also time and effort.

3. Designate a TV/movie night each week

Book at least one night a week to watch your favorite TV shows or movies that have caught your interest. It might be tempting to watch everything, especially in the age of streaming apps, but distancing your views can turn a lonely activity into a fun hangout with your friends.

This can be much cheaper than going to the movies as popcorn, soda, and other popular snacks are usually much more expensive than buying them at the grocery store and making them yourself.

4. Ride a bicycle whenever possible

Cycling has many benefits beyond the body and mind - it's already generally much cheaper than driving a vehicle or using public transport.

Going to work, running errands or just exploring the city - cycle short trips that don't require carrying a lot of luggage. You can install a basket, of course, but that would only be enough for a bag of medium-sized goods or supplies at most.

5. Create a mini bookcase

Encourage your neighbors to help you form a mini library that will be shared by all. Collect the books you have lying around the house and ask others for the same. Set aside a dedicated space for books and arrange them neatly.

When everything is ready, establish a rule that the borrower should leave a book whenever he wants to borrow it from the library. This way, you will keep the number of books while increasing their diversity. You will also be able to enjoy new titles without having to buy them yourself.

For a more hyggeligt experience, put comfortable sofas and armchairs in the library so that visitors have a place where they can hang out and read together.

6. Attend outdoor movie screenings

Open-air cinemas are very popular during the summer in several cities. Compared to watching movies in traditional theaters, doing it outdoors tends to be a cheaper, but still fun, way to spend time with loved ones, friends and family.

To make this a hyggeligt outing, you should make the most of its less formal setting. Spending hours in an open field and under the stars could be quite relaxing or romantic, depending on who you are. You can also bring food and drinks with you so you can have a mini picnic while watching the movie.

7. Exchange gifts using current items that are no longer in use

Do you have something in the basement that you've stored there for future use, but haven't had a reason to get it out since? Or maybe someone gave you an electric kettle but you already have one in the first place. Rather than waiting for an opportunity when you might find some use, why not invite your family and friends for a simple get-together where you can trade all the items you're not using at all?

Such parties can be quite hyggeligt because of all the good humor and fun times it could bring to everyone who attends them. You might think you could just sell the stuff on a garage clearance sale, flea market, or somewhere on the internet. However, none of these options can provide you with a hyggeligt experience.

In addition to getting yourself something that would be useful to you, an exchange will help clear your home of the unnecessary things you have in there. A clean home with minimal clutter is considered a prerequisite for a Hygge-filled home.

8. Complete DIY projects

Challenge yourself with DIY projects that you can use to decorate your home or workplace, or to give gifts to loved ones. Compared to the pre-made ones that are normally sold in stores, DIY items tend to be much, much cheaper. However, keep in mind that you need to invest your time instead of turning a project into a success.

Aside from cute little trinkets and artwork, try making homemade beauty products from scratch. Just make sure you look for a recipe that comes with a guarantee from others that you could easily follow.

If you're not willing to risk your hair or skin given your skills in DIY projects, choose to make your cleaning products instead. With the right set of ingredients and well-written instructions, you may be able to make dish detergents, stain removers, odor absorbers, and other useful home supplies that also come with your favorite scents.

DIY clothing projects can be quite hyggeligt too. Normally, people do this by knitting sweaters, scarves, and other ideal clothing for the cold season. However, you are free to try other sewing or weaving techniques that best suit your skill level and personal style.

9. Shop smarter

Living frugally doesn't mean you have to settle for what is the cheapest. Instead, it requires you to be smarter when it comes to whether or not to purchase a particular item. This way, you can be sure you are getting the best value for money.

Hygge also promotes quality over quantity in everything you do. Therefore, instead of buying something that would break after a couple of uses - this prompts you to buy a replacement - opt for something that could last for a longer period, even with regular use.

Finding, saving, and using shopping coupons could also help you save money. Through these, you will keep yourself from paying full price or get an extra item for a lower price or sometimes for free!

Keep in mind, however, that using coupons, as well as buying a discounted item, could only be considered a sign of frugal living if the item you want to buy is something you need or want. If your reason for buying it is mainly due to the alleged savings you would make, what you are doing goes against the principles of Hygge.

10. **Learn how to repair and maintain the things you use frequently**

Equipping yourself with this type of skill would help you save a lot of money every year. Since learning how to perform major repairs can take a long time, you need to focus on troubleshooting and doing minor repairs and maintenance work first.

Chapter 5: Benefits of Welcoming Happiness and Well-being

Denmark has long been at the top of the list of the happiest countries in the world, to the point of being called "the superpower of happiness". For years it has been at the top of the World Happiness Report commissioned by the United Nations (in 2017 it was ranked second after its Norwegian cousins) and Monocle magazine has repeatedly crowned Copenhagen the most liveable city in the world.

But what is the secret of the Scandinavian country? To answer this question, studies were conducted by universities, trade unions and journalists and the Happiness Research Institute was founded, a research institute that analyzes the well-being and quality of life of the Danes trying to identify the causes to create a model to be exported to the rest of the world. At first glance, the reason for well-being could be identified in the happiness of its people.

The Danes are encouraged to bear the high tax burden because what they receive from the state is directly proportional to the high taxes. A little as if, by paying them, they bought their well-being. However, as we dig deeper, the truth is enriched with new factors. To express in one word this typical feeling of happiness, the Danes even have a term, Hygge, a word that encompasses a set of elements that, combined, generate a widespread state of well-being that cannot be explained, but experienced.

The origin of the word is traced back to a Norwegian term meaning "well-being", but there are those who claim that it comes from "hug" or "hug". For others, however, it derives from "hygga", a term of the Norwegian language that stands for "consular". Interestingly, however diverse the origins of the word are, the meanings are all important elements of the Hygge philosophy. In his book "Hygge The Danish Way to Happiness", Meik Wiking, director of Happiness Research Institute of Copenhagen, tries to give us a more precise definition:
"Hygge is linked to an intimate, soft atmosphere and an experience rather than objects. It is being with the people we love. It is the feeling of being at home, of being safe, of being protected from the world and therefore of being able to let your guard down. Maybe just talking about the big or small things in life, enjoying a quiet and peaceful company or sipping a cup of tea alone."

Denmark has promoted the draft of the application for registration of Hygge as a UNESCO World Heritage Site. By adding Hygge to the list of intangible cultural heritages, we want to officially recognize its value as a real "antidote" to the anxieties of our time. The Danish group that is carrying out the bid project hopes that the benefits of the Hygge approach can spread even more and that Hygge can be experienced in a truly authentic way, giving a pinch of (Danish) happiness to the whole world. Among the experts involved in achieving this milestone are Meik Wiking - Founder and CEO of the Happiness Research Institute and Professor Jeppe Trolle Linnet, an anthropologist, who has studied the phenomenon in depth.

Serotonin

There is a close link between serotonin and happiness. Nutrition is often questioned, but increasing its levels with food may not be easy. Our happiness doesn't just depend on what surrounds us. It also contains biological factors such as hormones and neurotransmitters such as serotonin. This important molecule is responsible for our feelings of satisfaction, optimism and, more precisely, happiness. If your blood level is high, your mood is better; conversely, depression is accompanied by a decrease in their level.

It is no coincidence that most modern antidepressant drugs work by increasing the amount of serotonin available to brain cells. The genes that influence the serotonin levels in our brain depend on the action of two genes:

- The first (5-Httlpr) determines its distribution. There are two variants, one of which is associated with greater satisfaction with one's life;
- The second (Mao-A) controls its degradation. One of its variants is associated with the risk of forms of aggression; in women, low levels of expression of this variant are associated with a greater feeling of happiness. Genetic factors are not the only ones able to regulate the levels of this molecule.

Does altruism make you happy? Neuroscience says yes. At the brain level, the interplay between generosity and happiness is measurable. The intention is sufficient to produce detectable neural changes. We have heard this many times from people engaged in good causes: I receive more than I give. Now a study by neuro economists brings new evidence to support the thesis that altruism makes you happier, even when it comes to small actions. Even the simple promise to act selflessly is enough to trigger a change in the neurons of our minds. Conversely, those who move only by looking at their interest are scrutinized by less happy scientists.

Philippe Tobler and Ernst Fehr of the Department of Economics at the University of Zurich, in collaboration with researchers from other countries, subjected 50 volunteers to magnetic resonance imaging. They had been promised a certain amount of money in a few weeks and everyone had to think about how to use it, for whom (neighbor or stranger?), in what form and similar questions. Of the group, half were committed to giving, while the other was aimed at satisfying their needs and wants.

DEDICATED BRAIN AREAS- Three brain areas observed while the 50 subjects performed their respective tasks were the mechanical temporal junction (which is the area of empathy, where beneficial acts towards others are processed), the ventral striatum (associated with the feeling of happiness), the orbit cortex (which is where we weigh the pros and cons of making a decision). The results, the Swiss researchers note, offer a picture of the interplay between altruism and happiness. One of the unexpected observations is that there is no dose-dependent link between generosity and happiness. "You don't have to sacrifice yourself as a martyr to feel more satisfied," Tobler says. «Being a little more generous is enough. The simple promise to act selflessly activates the brain area of altruism and intensifies the relationship with happiness. It is truly remarkable that the intention already generates a neural change before the action is truly accomplished."

STOP THINKING?- It follows that the promise to behave selflessly can be used as a strategy to strengthen this commitment on the one hand and only to feel happier on the other. Another researcher from the "So Young Park" team of the University of Lübeck (Germany) mentions the questions that the Zurich study leaves open: "Will it be possible to strengthen communication between the three areas of the brain? And if so, how? Then: does the effect last when used deliberately, that is if a person behaves generously just to feel happier?"

THE GIFT, SOCIAL BASIS - Professor Alberto Oliverio, professor of Psychobiology at La Sapienza University in Rome, makes a brief comment: "The appearance of the gift is as old as the world. An aspect inherent in socialization because the meaning is to be accepted by the other. A feeling of a reward, reward or pleasure is linked to specific brain structures and acts as a reinforcement of our being, the basis of our social life."

More optimism

Optimism and pessimism are two qualities that characterize us humans in an extremely general way. At first glance, both can bring advantages and disadvantages. The optimist shows greater proactivity, but may run the risk of underestimating difficulties and dangers, thus acting instinctively and recklessly. The pessimist, on the other hand, can take an extremely cautious attitude and, overwhelmed by negative thoughts, risks missing out on good opportunities. It is a simplification. In reality, optimism and pessimism are not just two attitudes towards the future, the decisions to be made or the difficulties to be faced. They are also, as sociologists point out, "two different ways of relating to oneself and to other human beings."

We can identify two types of optimism:

- *A foolish optimism:* it has to do with naivety, with overconfidence in others, with a systematic underestimation of risks and dangers. It is typical of someone who is convinced that "things will settle down", that "sooner or later everything will have to go well". But then, if the situation gets worse and things don't work out, disillusionment, frustration, anger and cynicism will take the place of this blind and foolish optimism.

- A realistic optimism: it is typical of those who have the clear awareness of living in an imperfect and chaotic world, where difficulties are the order of the day; but that does not mean that he succumbs to negativity and pessimism. Indeed, try to face everything with courage, strength, decision.

What I will briefly analyze is the second type of optimism, the realistic one. What are the main characteristics of what we might call intelligent optimism? Optimists are not bothered by difficulties. The philosopher Karl Popper described human life as "a constant and incessant solution of problems". In small or large projects that we carry out every day, we necessarily encounter difficulties. As American psychologist Alan Loy McGinnis suggests in his essay The Force of Optimism, optimists are successful because they see themselves as problem solvers: when an attempt fails, they simply choose another path.

There is always a different possibility of achieving the goal: this is what optimists think, drawing on the different alternatives they have in mind to achieve the desired result. They try, they try and experiment until a solution turns out to be truly effective. At times the difficulties are such as to induce us to give up on a project that is close to our hearts. But even in such situations, realistic optimism can be of great help. Here is an example. Julio Iglesias played football at a professional level when a car accident paralyzed him for over a year, definitively compromising his career.

To ease the boredom of long days in the hospital, a nurse brought him a guitar. The rest is history. Optimists know how to give their thoughts a positive direction. Our attitude towards life events is not accidental. It is the result of a mixture of personal characteristics, environmental influences, examples, education, culture. All these elements are important, but they do not have the power to condition our attitudes. Cognitive psychologists argue that directing one's thoughts towards optimism rather than pessimism is a conscious choice. Obviously we can't always change events, turning them in our favor.

However, we always have the concrete possibility to change our interpretation of the events that happen to us. We have the power to control our thoughts, channeling them towards a positive tone, to produce beneficial effects on our emotions and moods. Philosopher William James said: "The greatest discovery of my generation is that human beings can change their lives by changing mental attitudes." Governing the course of our thoughts, interrupting and blocking the negative ones in the bud and nurturing those oriented towards realistic positivity, can prove to be an effective strategy to improve the quality of our life overall.

Optimists develop an internal locus of control. Each of us has a locus of control, that is, a point of control, which can be internal or external. Pessimists tend to attribute everything that happens to them to external causes, thus manifesting a predominantly external place of control. Optimists, on the other hand, believe they can be in full control of their own life, feeling responsible for their success, both professionally and personally. In this way, they demonstrate that they have an internal locus of control, which allows them to manage problems and critical situations more effectively, to achieve their goals and to better cope with efforts and fatigue. If the place of internal control is a personal feature, it undoubtedly needs to be continually nurtured and developed.

They are therefore constantly oriented towards improving their skills and specific skills, to have greater control over the results they intend to achieve. Optimists know how to recharge and renew themselves at regular intervals. Optimism needs to be recharged continuously. If new energy is not continuously fed, our organism deteriorates and disintegrates. The same dynamic concerns the area of relationships, from professional to personal. If you do not take care and attention, the relationships with time become more lukewarm, they lose solidity until they disintegrate. They need constant energy recharges. This also applies to optimism.

As Alan Loy McGinnis points out, "it is those who consciously or unconsciously take steps to neutralize personal entropy that keeps the optimism alive, and keeps the enthusiasm alive over the years." For example, they bond with positive and successful people, possibly avoiding those who tend to complain continuously by emitting negativity; they seek to meet and meet new people, from whom they can learn and enrich themselves intellectually, emotionally and spiritually; they go beyond the established habits in their daily life, making small or big changes in their lives. These are just some simple tricks, which can significantly contribute to injecting new energy into one's existence, nurturing a positive and confident attitude.

Optimists develop the ability to enjoy the present. Being centered on the present does not mean having any memory of the past or having no future planning skills. Rather, it means knowing how to savor the present moment, the here and now. Optimists have developed the ability to enjoy the small and simple things that our daily life offers us: the smell of coffee at breakfast, the smile of a loved one, the feeling of well-being after a run in the park, the sight of the sun at sunset, a dinner with family or partner. Common situations, too often considered obvious. Optimists can value them, appreciate them and consider them gifts to be grateful for, savoring in the present the sensations that such simple moments are capable of arousing. Our way of thinking and acting is the result of a choice. The decision to go towards optimism, that is to seize opportunities, to trust, to value the positive aspects of situations, to look to the future with hope, is a decision that we can all make. So why not try?

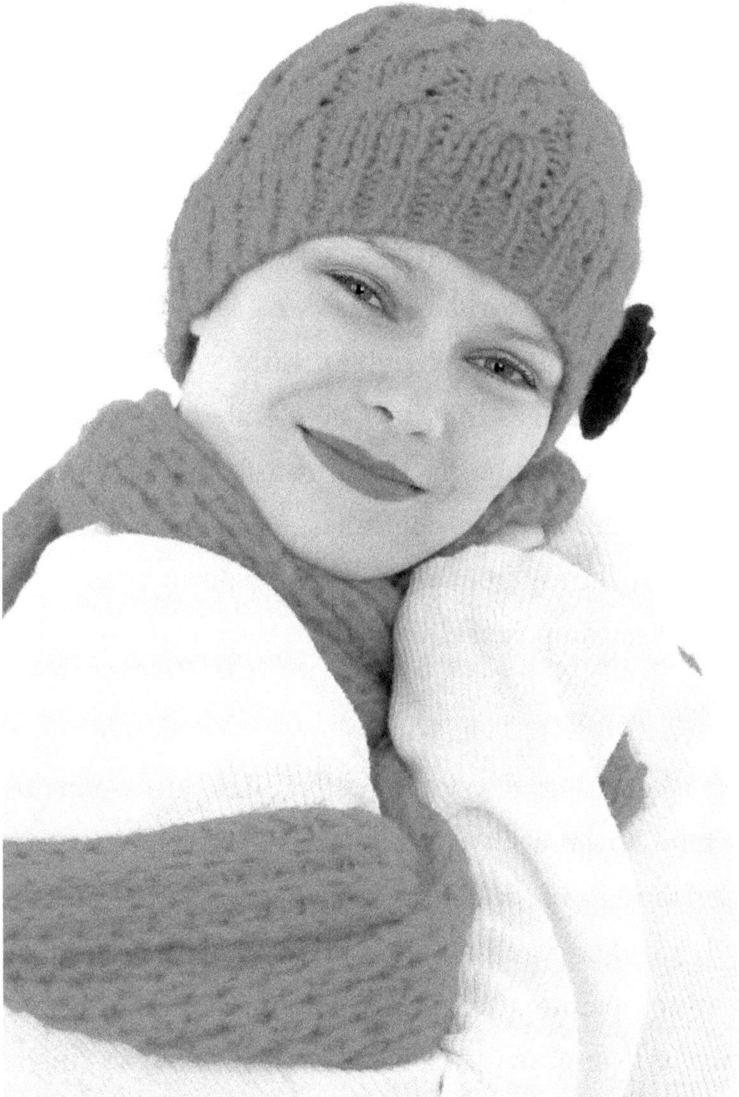

Eliminate the stress

There is a widespread idea that stress is a product of modernity, a side effect of the hectic lifestyle of recent years. Of course, today everything runs fast and burns in an instant, but it is also true that the contemporary frenzy has mostly become the normal speed of the world, to which we have adapted better than we think. Furthermore, all human history is characterized by discoveries or changes that have accelerated the way of life and man has always adapted to these transformations. This means that the nervous tension continues, which characterizes those suffering from stress from another internal source. Stress always arises from self-imposed obligations.

Setting a goal or developing a project are good tests to understand how much we can increase or decrease stress, that is to understand if we are acting in an elastic and therefore natural or rigid and therefore pathological way. In the second case, we will tend to operate according to schematic times and methods that we self-impose ourselves to respect. The higher the expectations, the stricter these programs become, the more stress increases.

At the same time, the shadow of failure, negative self-judgment and contempt lengthens as the course of things deviates from the predetermined path. The stronger the diktat to reach the set goal, the more stress is guaranteed. The reason why we feel bad therefore depends on our mental attitude. The problem is that this behavior, if repeated, involves not only the mind, but also the body.

There are behaviors we can adopt to get out of this impasse. If there is a hyper-rational way of thinking that fills us with stress, there is also the alternative: it consists of giving priority to creativity, imagination and above all to the search for the essential. This is what most of all saves us from stress. How to do it? Here are some practical tips:

- *Read the signals of the body and the environment and adapt.* Learn to read the signals coming from the body and the reality around you (special coincidences, unexplained events, instinctive rejection or attraction) and try to follow them without asking yourself why. There is emotional intelligence in anyone who can interpret these signs much better than our minds.

- *Accept your contradictions.* Do not give events a single reading: everything that happens has a wider meaning than what we attribute to it. A failure is not just a failure:

it is also an evolutionary stage that somehow had to be done.

- *Trust your imagination.* During the day, carve out a small space, close your eyes and let yourself go to the fantasies, welcoming the images that are formed without comments. The imagination, when released from prepackaged dreams (like prince charming, or becoming rich and famous), will give you valuable and great suggestions, coming from a new perspective.

- *Don't struggle with events.* From time to time let things take their course without trying to control them. Leave it to chance or wait and see what happens.

- *You don't care to understand.* Do not insist on finding a logical sense or a material cause for everything: life is not rational. If you don't force it into your schemes, it will reveal unexpected implications.

- *Eliminate preconceptions.* Try to "observe" your beliefs as if you were another person: you will be surprised to discover how many ideas, deeply rooted in you, are groundless or no longer valid at the moment you are living. Remember that our beliefs are always the result of learning: they are never entirely "ours".

The benefits of gratitude

What exactly is gratitude and how does it affect our mood? Let's start with an example. Have you ever noticed the faces of the Olympic athletes during the awards ceremony? Those who receive a bronze medal seem happier than those who take the silver home. Because? It's easy to say: winning a medal is always nice, even if it is bronze; losing the title of champion, perhaps for a long time, leaves a bad taste in the mouth. So the bronzes are grateful to be on the podium, while the silver still gnaws. It is a sensation and it is essentially a psychological matter.

There are several studies on this, and all of them have found that practicing gratitude offers several benefits.

Here are the main ones:
1. makes you a better person;
2. enriches friendships;

3. happiness increases;
4. makes life more beautiful for people close to you;
5. it helps to be less depressed, anxious, envious, lonely and neurotic.

Furthermore, according to research results from Sonja Lyubomirsky, a professor of psychology at the University of California, gratitude is one of the common characteristics of the happiest people. Keeping a gratitude journal is a practice suggested by all happiness "experts", and even if I thought it was nonsense, after living it I have to admit that no, it isn't.

It is a treatment with deep scientific roots. Gratitude helps reduce stress, increases positive perceptions and reduces negative perceptions. According to scholars, it is linked to mental health and to the satisfaction perceived by one's life. To experience this practice, I added a question to my daily journal ritual to be answered every day: "What are you grateful for today?"

I discovered that there are things I take for granted, but they are the ones that most affect my mood, and consequently my approach to everyday life. For example, some of the things I've been grateful for in the past few weeks, but never would have noticed if I hadn't taken a moment, realizing it, a lunch with my wife, an invitation to her wedding from a friend I haven't heard in a long time, a compliment from a former colleague, a comment from a person who printed my e-book to give to his daughter, a missed accident, a book that was suggested to me and loved, my daughter who hears me going down the stairs to have breakfast and runs towards me.

All things that, if you take a minute to write them, like to say, come to life in your mind, "amplify" your memory and perpetuate the happiness that those moments have already given you. It takes little, you will say. And it's true: it doesn't take much. The amazing thing is that this little one works. Look, it's normal for you to be skeptical: I was too skeptical at the beginning and I still struggle to write a few lines when that time of day comes.

However, I have found that taking a minute to accomplish the things we are thankful for gives you a refill of happiness whose effects are more noticeable in the long term than in the short term. The sense of repeated happiness that comes from expressing your gratitude helps you find the right rhythm. It gives rise to an unstoppable force within you that spurs you to follow your heart, to venture into the most diverse follies and continue, continue, continue to do everything to complete your project. Without ever stopping, giving life to that state of mind called "flow" by the psychologist Mihály Csíkszentmihályi, and which involves serious fun in doing what you do, to the point of losing the perception of time and dedicating oneself to creating something to be truly proud of.

Traveling makes you happy

Can a journey make you happy? Yes, and not only: here are the travel advantages that we absolutely must know! Those who love to travel tend to be very happy: it is not fiction, but pure reality and a scientific study conducted by Cornell University confirms this. A trip would seem to have many positive effects on a person's life and far outweigh the happiness that a shopping spree can give. Spending money on a leisure trip is the best thing to do for your health. Here are the advantages of traveling! The beneficial effects of travel: what are they? Those returning from a leisure trip usually tend to be calmer and less stressed. Happiness that, as reported by science itself, nothing else can give you.

The study conducted by the university professor of psychology, Thomas Gilovich, wanted to title this experiment "A wonderful life: experiential consumption and pursuit of happiness" or tends to emphasize the importance of spending one's money on a life experience to find happiness, rather than spending your money on an item. This is because a trip would greatly increase the sense of happiness. There are many advantages that a trip can offer: - Stimulate curiosity because you discover new places, new people and new habits. -It is a great way to get to know not only the world, but also oneself: a journey, in fact, often and willingly invites us to overcome all limits.-

Eliminate stress and this is possible because breaking away from the routine now and then is more than good for physical and mental health. A way to regenerate your energies! -A trip gives you new experiences and even new friends: those who tend to travel become more sociable and open to getting to know anyone. Also, to be able to travel in complete tranquility we can opt for apps to download on your smartphone that allow us to be better organized even during our vacation!

94

Chapter 6: Simple Ways to Practice Hygge

Used to living in a wonderful but hostile environment for long periods of the year, the Danes have learned to carve out little moments of happiness and serenity every day, especially during the long, dark and harsh winter. Spending an evening with loved ones, or reading a book by candlelight, having a drink and eating something together without being connected to the net is Hygge. Spending time in a relaxing and comfortable environment where you feel perfectly at ease, free from pressures, duties and stresses is Hygge.

How to practice Hygge if you are not Danish? Although it is a practically untranslatable word, it is understood with little effort that Hygge cannot be defined uniquely. It is what makes you feel good and at the same time it is the deep commitment to achieve serenity. In light of these assumptions, there i as many happiness as there are individuals who seek them and there is no universally valid recipe.

Hygge is the search for the here - and - now or the ability to fully experience a moment or situation without being simultaneously distracted (intellectually and emotionally) by other thoughts or worries. Creating small personal rituals to repeat when we need to recharge our energies can be a perfect first step towards conquering Hygge. Showering as soon as you get home after work, wearing comfortable clothes, and having a cup of tea or herbal tea after dinner are likely actions many of us do every day, without paying adequate attention to what we are doing. Hygge is a state of mind, the ability to fully experience the perfection of small moments that can put us in tune with ourselves and with the world around us.

American anthropologists have been struck by the "hyggeligt" interactions and the fact that no one tries to be center stage. It is a time when everyone takes off their mask and leaves difficulties behind the door trying to appreciate the power of the presence of others. There are mountains of research that support the importance of social bonds for well-being. Feelings received and given to others are the meaning and purpose of life. Social bonds can increase longevity, reduce stress, and even boost our immune systems. The researchers also found that Denmark's egalitarianism plays an important role. For example, a 2009 study by Robert Biswas-Diener found that while wealthy Americans and Danes are equally happy.

Here are five "Hygge" rules you may want to apply to your life:

1. **Be yourself**. Let your guard down. Don't try to prove what you are not.

2. **Forget about disputes**. Prefer light-hearted and balanced discussions. Good food and company.

3. **Think you're a team member**. Work with family or group members and help them prepare dinner.

4. **See the Hygge factor as a refuge from the outside world**. A place where everyone can relax and open their hearts without judging and being judged, regardless of what's going on in your life. For better or for worse, this place is sacred and problems can be left out.

5. **Remember that the Hygge factor is limited in time**. Hygge can be difficult for a non-Dane. Being center stage, bragging or complaining, being too negative and trying to be present without arguing?

These are very difficult behaviors to implement, but the rewards could be huge. It's an incredible feeling to share these moments smoothly with the people you like the most. Let's see now how to practice Hygge.

- Decorate your home with natural elements. Simple furniture that respects the inhabitants and guests, without exceeding the superfluous. In practice, the synthesis of the Nordic style: lots of wood and natural materials, plants, large windows to let in light and bright colors. Each choice follows the desire to surround yourself with nature and harmony, to experience moments of pleasure and sharing.

- Create the right, comfortable and soft atmosphere. To achieve a relaxing atmosphere, you can play with the lighting by alternating lamps in various parts of the house, preferably with warm lights. Placing one at the entrance will make the return after a long day of work sweeter, while the light from the living room lampshade, if kept low and soft, will make the room more inviting.

- Live in the moment (and turn off your smartphone). Be present to yourself, here and now, say the Hygge poster. Create a place to stop, listen to music or read. Orient the reading lamp, order your records to have them at hand, arrange your favorite chair in the most comfortable way. Keep a straw basket with wraparound scarves, gloves, and wool socks next to you to cover yourself in cold weather. If there was a fireplace, it would be perfect indeed: a flickering flame to watch to completely relax.

- Read a book (or travel guide). The key to Hygge is to feel good about yourself - so take some time for yourself. Time for what? Reading, for example. To sink into an armchair when it is raining or snowing outside, create the right atmosphere, raise the thermostat ball and finally start that novel. If you are one of the people who love to travel, I always recommend reading a travel guide. If Hygge feels good, nothing is more Hygge than fantasizing about the next trip from the heat of your home.

- Welcome friends to your home. Invite family and friends for a casual dinner or a new tradition, be it board games or a movie forum. One guest or many, what matters is sharing, being together, telling each other. We often go out in the evening and end up in a club with such loud music that, in addition to sipping a cocktail, we spend a good part of the evening screaming to communicate with friends, or worse, to slide the phone. Hygge is not about retiring in your living room with trusted friends, background music and chat. Without ulterior motives or organized activities. Tell your day, tell your travels, have a good time. Do you have a fireplace? Better!

- Dedicated to hobbies and passions. Create a DIY corner for decorations. Nothing is missing: scissors, glue, colored papers, colors, salvaged items. You can make simple decorations following the seasons of the year or according to your inspiration: for example wreaths with flowers and branches with ribbons and balls. Create a space for children too. It will be fun to create something together and convey the care and love for the environment in which they live.

- The Lego. Playing with Legos is Hygge. In fact, it's something that makes you feel good, that you do at home, that you enjoy, that you can do it yourself or not. And above all, it's Danish like Hygge: the company that produces the best-selling bricks in the world was founded in Denmark by Ole Kirk Kristiansen in 1916, and in Denmark there is Legoland, the unmissable theme park for Lego lovers! The word Lego itself comes from the Danish "leg godt", which means "play well".

- Create your nest. Step by step, the house becomes more and more a nest. Choose the most suitable fabrics to obtain a cocooning effect, a cocoon. If in summer fresh fabrics and light colors prevail, in winter they will be soft and hairy with darker shades, while the carpets will be thick and shaggy for walking freely with bare feet.

- Spread the time in the kitchen. Cooking with others and for others, rediscovering the pleasure of preparing food slowly. Pull out your grandmother's cookbook and invite a friend for homemade pasta or traditional dessert. Better to have all the tools insight, so everyone can contribute without having to wonder where they are. If there is a large island, it will be fun to walk around it between passes during preparation. While waiting for the kitchen, lots of chat and good wine to taste in your most precious glasses. You will turn those hours into a special afternoon.

- Stay in touch with nature. Gardening can relax you and give you a home full of greenery. Each leaf can give color and energy to your life: you can choose larger plants like ficus or kenzia. Have fun creating elegant green corners with succulents, such as sansevieria to combine with ceramic jars with small and large cacti.

- Back home. We all have a home to return to, and nothing is more Hygge than being with family - holidays are the most Hygge season of the year. Sure, Christmas can be stressful, but coming home for a weekend and being pampered by mom or dad, or grandparents, or boyfriend/girlfriend is always a good idea. It doesn't matter where you feel at home - go there for a few days. And if it's far away, book your flight in advance.

- The classic hot drink. It's a bit cliché, no doubt, but in Hygge ABC is the classic hot drink to drink on the sofa. But put a bit of imagination: you don't live only on decaffeinated sachets and cappuccinos. A zabajone, a delicious hot chocolate with cream, an infusion of ginger and turmeric, a black or red tea, chamomile made by you with fresh flowers ... and who knows if he loves you.

As long as both drinks are warm and reassuring, it's Hygge.

- Take a sauna. In Scandinavia, the home sauna is often a reality. In other countries it is more difficult for your apartment to have a wooden environment where you can throw cold water on hot stones, or where you can get massaged by expert hands. Ok, Hygge is also about booking a hotel with a sauna and spending an evening of absolute relaxation.

- Take a walk in the snow. Maybe you got the idea that Hygge stays home doing nothing. That's partly true, but we don't want you to get lazy: Hygge is also going out for a walk in the snow, or in the cold of the city at night, when no one is around and the traffic is quiet. Finally back in your home, hibernating, your apartment will look much more Hygge than before! Although it doesn't look like a Danish cottage.

- To sleep. Great for spending time in an armchair or with friends by candlelight. But too often there is an underestimated Hygge activity: and it is sleep. But not your normal night's sleep. The extraordinary nap that we allow ourselves, the one under 10 kilos of blankets on the sofa, perhaps absentmindedly watching TV or listening to a good record. Alone or accompanied. Lazy is Hygge.

- Finally, go to Denmark! The radical solution: organize a trip to Denmark to ask the Danes directly. Maybe Hygge is something that cannot be explained in words, and it is necessary to go to the source to find out how it "works". At worst, you will have had a great vacation!

Chapter 7: How to Spend a Danish Day

While most Americans start and end their days in a:
- ✓ dead race: drink coffee and, if you're lucky, have breakfast to get the kids to school while dodging traffic and getting to work on time;
- ✓ catch up on work-work-work emails;
- ✓ take the kids to the activities;
- ✓ eating take-out or leftovers on the go;
- ✓ collapse in bed.

This is the opposite of having a Danish day! The emphasis is not on performing tasks or ticking off items in a list; the emphasis is on living a present and happy life. Instead of focusing on instant gratification or fulfilling consumer fantasies, the Danes try to experience relationships with people and their environment. Let's imagine how we could immerse ourselves in a Danish day of Hygge: simple, practical, interactive and happy.

Good morning

After a wonderfully rested night, you wake up to light candles around the house, giving off a soft, warm glow that gently accompanies you through the day. The house is tidy and simple, organized but comfortable, with just enough of what you need without the clutter of conspicuous consumption. Make a generous cup of cocoa - or a rich, dark coffee - and eat a thick, comforting slice of rugbrød (Danish rye bread). Or perhaps a large bowl of porridge is more appropriate to fuel your day, complete with whole grains, some sliced fruit, and a handful of chopped nuts sprinkled all over. If it's a weekday, be prepared to go to your workspace for five or six hours.

If you are Danish, you are most likely working in a position that offers you a solid and stable life. Remember, Dane's post-high school education is free, which leads to a less competitive and more collaborative workplace. Remember that work should be a place that satisfies your need to be creative. We should all be productive, contribute to the world around us and why we only care about accumulating money or status! In Denmark, the gap between the rich and the less rich is the lowest in the world; everyone has the opportunity to live a safe and happy life. If you were to lose your job, the government would help you - up to 90 percent of your salary would be provided for about four years as a pillow until you find another opportunity. The job is satisfying because it is a career of choice, and your workspace is almost as inviting as your home. It doesn't seem like a chore because it's not the only important thing in your life, as your supervisor and colleagues know! Work is a part of a full life and you don't take it home with you. Instead, leave in the afternoon, ready to enjoy the rest of what life has to offer.

Good afternoon

It's afternoon and it's the perfect time to spend some outdoors. At home you have large windows that allow you to soak up the sun during the long summer days or enjoy the snow and storms that linger during the short winter days. Plan to spend some time outdoors each day, in communion with nature. Maybe you decide to go to the park, where you will always meet someone you know, maybe a friend or a neighbor. Maybe you'll meet them there for an afternoon picnic if the weather cooperates. It doesn't matter: the Danish climate is always unpredictable, but you are always prepared. A picnic in the park could easily turn into an afternoon spent in a cafe. Either way, you will probably spend time with friends at the bar. It's the Danish thing to do!

You jump on your bike - nine out of ten Danes have one, often use it daily - doing exercises that don't feel like exercises as you walk to the bar. You have already made your simple lunch: a smørrebrød of liver pate, herring or roast pork. Now, coffee is the time for a nice cup of coffee or cocoa and, of course, a delicious dessert, perhaps a pastry or a large piece of cake. Fulfilling sweets are a part of Hygge practice - anything that walking and cycling and getting in touch with nature gives you one more reason to indulge. You meet friends, a nice intimate group of three or four where you can talk about your job, the weather, the kids, whatever strikes you. The important part of every day is socializing and being with your friends. One of your friends carries her newborn in a stroller and since the weather is nice, you all sit outside while you share thoughts, coffee and cake. Your friend is enjoying her generous maternity leave; has a very fulfilling whole year to spend with her son before returning to work. Everyone shares this human opportunity to feed a newborn, a benefit of the Danish welfare system.

Once your pleasant break at the bar is over, head to the market, where you go to buy some fresh produce and other ingredients for dinner. This is a significant part of the day, something you do most days because cooking and eating together is a very important part of everyday life. Furthermore, the practice of Hygge emphasizes promoting local relationships and contributing to the good in the world - shopping at the market is an excellent way to satisfy all of these elements. Build relationships with farmers, owners, and purchase the healthiest, freshest food you can find to feed yourself and your family. It's not about imaginative and fussy ingredients, when you come home from your forays, you decide to take some time to take care of yourself. Maybe light some candles in the bathroom and take a relaxing bath before making dinner. If it's summer, maybe you sit outside with another cup of coffee and enjoy the afternoon sunlight with your card or puzzle, or just spend some time relaxing with your thoughts. Go ahead; this is the meaning of hyggeligt. It takes some charging to recharge! If it's winter, maybe you light a fire and wrap yourself in a blanket in your cozy hyggekrog (Hygge corner) and grab a good book to read. Whatever you decide, it's never a bad idea to spend some time taking care of yourself, indulging in some relaxing moments of your choice.

Good evening

You are now ready to start making dinner. The family is now all at home - everyone knows that dinner is spent together and that friends are always welcome - and everyone, of age, contributes to the preparation and presentation of the meal. As this is a typical Danish day, you've decided to make something hearty and healthy, simple but full of comforting flavor. Perhaps you have decided to make stegtflaesk, one of the national dishes of the Danes, made up of some crispy pork and boiled potatoes with parsley cream sauce. Or maybe you are just channeling the spirit of Hygge and decide to make a ground stew with some meat and vegetables you bought at the market something simple that only takes a little time to prepare, then quite a bit time to cook while filling the home with comforting scents. This gives you time to talk to family and friends, make a hot drink or two, and set the table so everyone feels welcome and at ease. Surely the setting of the atmosphere is one of the fundamental aspects of Hygge, and you like to present a table with beautiful crockery and/or flowers and/or decorative vases. The focus is not on the objects themselves, but rather on making the table an inviting and pleasant place to gather around. Of course, everyone has turned off their phones and put aside their tablets or laptops, because it's about spending time together and you like to present a table with beautiful crockery and/or flowers and/or decorative vases. The focus is not on the objects themselves, but rather on making the table an inviting and pleasant place to gather around. Of course, everyone has turned off their phones and put aside their tablets or laptops, because it's about spending time together.

Once dinner is ready, everyone gets together and eats, family style, savoring the simple pleasure of dining together on good, fresh foods that are home-cooked and eaten as a family. This may be one of the most crucial pieces of the Danish happiness puzzle - this kind of special family time isn't spared for special occasions. These times are daily occurrences, promoting a culture of kindness, generosity and gratitude. It could even be suggested that the high rates of happiness and low rates of poverty and crime are due to the simple fact that breaking bread together is one of the most powerful unifiers within any society. Some would say that once lost, there is a kind of friendship that is badly missed. Hence, the Danish emphasis on after dinner, when it gets dark, it will be late in the summer; in winter, twilight comes early enough - you gather in your cozy space, with an intimate room for everyone. Maybe you decide to play some friendly games together, or it's time for casual conversation. If you and your partner or spouse are alone, you can decide to watch a movie together, snuggle up in a warm blanket in front of a fire or bathe in a candlelight. Maybe you're on your own for the evening, which gives you a chance to go back to your hyggekrog and spend a glorious couple of hours reading a wonderful book. Since your day has been spent enjoying every moment with no stress and no rush or with the feeling of never having time to do enough, you fall asleep easily and dream lightly of another beautiful hyggeligt day.

The Takeaway

Hygge itself is almost indefinable in English: for some, it indicates a lifestyle, as vaguely outlined above; for others it indicates a personal feeling of intimate comfort. For others, it indicates a mindset of being present at every moment of the day. The combination of all three will bring you closer to the Hygge experience on a typical Danish day. The reason for Hygge's recent popularity seems to need little explanation: In a world haunted by stress and demands, Hygge represents a return to something simpler, happier, and ultimately more fulfilling.

Certainly, Danish society is set for Hygge, with its generous social status, equal and stable wages and a cultural penchant for work-life balance. Not only do Danes have the shortest workweek in Europe (around 35 hours for the most part), but they also have at least five weeks of paid vacation per year and mothers have paid maternity leave for a full year. There are also social safety nets of all kinds, from free college education to unemployment benefits that pay up to 90% of your salary for up to four years. Extreme poverty and homelessness are virtually unknown throughout Denmark and health care is nationalized and free. All this at the expense of taxpayers, of course, and the Danes pay the highest tax rates of almost all countries in the world (almost 60% in 2019). Still, most Danes don't complain about the high tax rate because of the social benefits everyone receives. It is a rare example of a truly egalitarian society where most people believe their country will be better off if everyone is educated, healthy and cared for when needed.

When we look around other Western countries, especially America, we see a huge gap between the very rich and the very poor, which does not exist in Denmark. The trade-off, as some might argue, is that you don't have the opportunity to get rich in Denmark; everyone is educated, salaries are comparable across the board. Raising one's status is not easy. A typical Danish response might be to suggest that happiness is not synonymous with wealth or status. The Danes have little to fear from the crime or other evils that societies with large wealth inequality face. These are just some of the social norms that give Danes little reason to change their current system.

If you are a woman in Danish society, you may even have a more beneficial view of this system. For many reasons, Danish women don't feel the pressure to get married. Their society is so egalitarian; women have the same education and opportunities as men. They have access to the same types of stable, well-paid jobs. Women don't have to rely on men for money or status. Second, with generous maternity leave and unemployment benefits, women can achieve a much greater work-life balance, especially when it comes to having and raising a family. This is one of the most important aspects of Danish culture that other Western countries would do well to consider.

Hence, Danish social systems are set up in line with the practice of Hygge! Living elsewhere, many do not necessarily enjoy the benefits and security of that particular national way of life. If it sounds like the Hygge lifestyle to you, it's still possible to introduce elements of Hygge into your daily routine with thoughtfulness and care. Who isn't attracted to a life of less stress, more awareness and pleasurable contentment? This is what it takes to start practicing Hygge: the desire to create an atmosphere conducive to comfort and calm, a focus on togetherness and family rather than work and status, and the belief that material wealth and consumer products are not equal to happiness. Rather, it is an inherent feeling that comes from leading a comforting life of self-care and well-being.

The checklist

Self-care is the key! Hygge means giving yourself permission to eliminate all your stresses and worries and make sure you are healthy and happy - only then can you help others be happy and healthy.
The atmosphere strengthens the mentality. Soft Lighting: Most Danes agree that without candlelight there can be no hyggeligt.

It is a must along with earthy and comfortable furniture, large windows whenever possible, simplicity of design and a minimum of clutter. Fewer things equal more life.

Simplicity, simplicity, simplicity! Hygge is about appreciating the simple pleasures of life: going outside, talking with friends, spending time in a bar, reading a good book, staying in the present and appreciating what you have.

Speaking of outdoor activities, go out every day. Fresh air and healthy exercise - riding a bike or playing in the park - are also key to cultivating the practice of Hygge. Nature should be an inspiration to enjoy every day.

Coffee culture is important throughout Europe, but it is certainly an important part of the Hygge lifestyle. It's about being with friends, enjoying hot drinks and tasty (read: sugary) foods. Cafes are the focus of the Danish day.

Markets are also significant. Kitchens are small and free in much of Europe in general and daily shopping at the local market is a way of life for many. It is a way to commune with others, to contribute to the community, and to provide healthy local food and goods for your family.

Make dinner at home and eat together - every day - or at least as often as practically possible. Turn off phones and other devices and make each night a holiday-worthy meeting.

Success is not defined by a material thing. Rather, success is about work-life balance, creativity and productivity in your life, comfort and happiness in your home.

Chapter 8: Hygge Away From Home

Holidays are especially important when it comes to Hygge and being able to use it for yourself. Christmas will be one of the main reasons for this school of thought, and you will find that there are different dishes and different ways to celebrate it based on where you come from. It is important to note that in Denmark and other countries around there, the Christmas season is not necessarily full of religion, but they like to have their traditions and it is often full of fun and a lot of great food. Of course, people in this area can get a little crazy sometimes too.

On each of the Sundays of Advent, which are the four Sundays that occur before December 25, many families will go out and have a snowball fight with each other, regardless of the weather. Everyone will drink many of the same things, such as glogg, which is a spiced red wine that is heated with raisins and almonds, and will eat pepper crackers, which is like a gingerbread cookie. Some families may even have some of their favorite recipes that they share during this time.

During the holidays there is always something fun to do. You can spend your time cooking all the awesome festive dishes or cookies and bars and more. There are terrines to prepare, fish to care for and beets to store. But while we're doing all this work, it's important to do it together, sharing time, stories and laughter. This is what brings Hygge into the mix.

In addition to celebrating Christmas, there is also a large festival known as Saint Lucia which is held on December 13th. This is a celebration that is meant to celebrate our life and good food. The girls will dress in white dresses and sing as they walk with lit candles. It is a beautiful celebration that brings many people together. This festival also drinks a lot of glogg and St. Lucia Buns, or sweet and mellow delicacies, are shared by all who are enjoying the festival.

Of course, Christmas evening will be one of the most important days of this festival. Dinner should start around six in the evening and will include a roast duck. The men are the ones who will be responsible for cooking the duck, and you will be able to see grills lined up in the neighborhood as the men work to roast the birds together, usually in groups, and drink some wine.

Many great dishes are celebrated in a Hygge Christmas. On the table you will find dishes such as roast pork, potatoes, sweet and sour red cabbage and a wide variety of vegetables. Desserts can range from biscuits and other treats, but cold rice pudding with a hot cherry sauce is also popular.

When everyone is full and has enough of the good food from this meal, it's time to sing and dance around the tree. This can last for some time as it continues until everyone is tired. So, it's time to hand out the gifts and open them.

While all of this seems to be enough to make the celebration's Hygge stand out, there's still more. You will still have time to spend with your family and friends. The next day many families are still together and will sometimes enjoy what is known as a buffet, which often includes open sandwiches with various toppings. This could be many different toppings, cured meats, cured salmon, or another seasoning. It will all end with some cheese and sweets to finish off the meal. Sometimes, the family extends it a little longer and takes a long walk together, to enjoy each other's company and whet their appetite before they go in and eat.

The best part about Hygge is that you can create some of your own traditions that go with the family during this time. You don't have to go and do everything as the Danes does. If you still see Christmas as a religious holiday, it's okay to celebrate those traditions as well and keep them. There are no hard and fast rules other than spending time and enjoying the company of others while eating good food and drinks and sharing some laughs and good memories. If your traditions fit all this, you are already taking a hyggeligt vacation and there is no need to change anything.

Holidays are one of the best times to see how Hygge is at work. You are already excited about all the good things to come and it's easy to feel happy and ready to take on the world when all that good food is cooking and you know your loved ones will run out in no time. Now, the trick is to take some of those good feelings from the holidays and time you spent with your family and learn how to spread it throughout the year.

Add Hygge all year round

Now that we've spent some time talking about how Hygge works during the holiday season, it's important to note that you can experience Hygge all year round. Most of us are familiar with the ideas and feelings that emerge during the Christmas season when we celebrate with family and friends. All that warmth that comes from being around people we love, all that gift, good food and happy moments. We know that feeling even though we haven't used Hygge in our lives so far. But what happens during the rest of the year? Do we just have to wait until the end of the year, when it's close to Christmas before we can relive it?

While Hygge is usually seen as a winter season idea, it's one you can use all year round. Most holidays and celebrations happen in the winter because people need a little more warmth and social moments when they are stuck inside with the cold all the time. But you can celebrate Hygge all year round. Even when it is warm outside and the weather is nice, you can feel comfortable no matter what time of year. Hygge is not reserved for a season or a holiday; it is meant to be enjoyed at any time of the year.

While you may have been thinking about the cold winter months when we were talking about some of these ideas, why couldn't you expand it to have a bonfire with the people you love in the winter, throw a barbecue, or go for a walk during the summer months?

There are many ways you can experience Hygge during the summer too. Some of the best examples you will find can be a lot of fun and will bring you closer to those you love, including having a barbecue, playing in the park with a pet, lighting candles at night or when others are finished, having a pool party, having a nice picnic with friends or take a long walk. If you find that it's been a while since you were last with some of the people you love, why not invite them over for dinner and enjoy each other's company. With Hygge, it doesn't have to be something complicated and will require a tremendous amount of planning; even just a simple lunch or dinner with the people you love will be enough for this.

Hygge is a great thing to add to some of your celebrations, especially during the winter months when you're often stuck inside and may not see people as often as you want, but that doesn't mean you can't use it in the rest of the world as well. When you learn to make Hygge a part of your life all year round.

Parenting and Hygge relationships

On a fundamental level, Hygge is a phenomenon that unites individuals. When we put ourselves on the right edge of our personality to enjoy each other's conversation, we begin to focus on each other in new and energetic ways. In a Hyggelig lifestyle, we tend to develop mutual affection, a sense of goodwill, and a strong bond in our relationships. Isolationists may claim otherwise, but we cannot live a normal, joyful life without our relationships and nothing else can help us achieve the goal as much as Hygge. On the off chance that you never knew about Hygge, you should seriously think that your relationships in life are enough, no more claims to improve. Nobody's perfect. Everyone has merits and demerits.

When you invest your free energy in the organization of others, whether you are their life partner, youth, guardian or siblings, would you say that you are there with them? If the direct answer is YES, then proceed as you did. However, in the fact that you feel your relationship leaves an opportunity to improve, or you feel something is missing, or there is an emotional emptiness, consider the different ways Hygge can enable you to be close to others. You will feel the difference in a few days.

Bride

On the off chance that there's ever a relationship that gives Hygge ample space, it's the spousal one. The sentimental estate is loaded with single minutes between you and your loved one. While you love these cozy occasions, remember the word Hygge and appreciate falling in time.

Young people/children

One of the reasons Denmark is such a happy place is that most of the children grew up with Hygge. When sending Hygge to your country, be sure to take the kids to the good times. Tell them about Hygge and then compose the environment with the goal that they can experience it for themselves. It may take some time for young people to understand the idea (as they do for adults), but they will stick to it once they start reaping its fruits.

Guardians and brothers

Likewise, since your youngsters can be educated about the Hygge lifestyle, it's never past the point where you can present similar ideas to your people and relatives. On the next occasion, when your whole family is as one, notice the concept of Hygge and what you have learned so far. You and your family will enjoy Hygge together on such a night and on all occasions to come.

Friends

Tell all your friends about Hygge and they are more likely not to overlook him. Hygge pervades the air anytime you know each other, so why not introduce him by his name? Next time, you are planning to meet dear newlyweds, recommend another bistro that you have discovered has incredible potential for Hygge. Abandon yourself to the occasion and appreciate the direct encounter of your meeting.

At that point, bring the lovely Hygge to their awareness. Tell them what you found out about Hygge, see their opinion on it. The bistro you're in will be an amazing down-to-earth place to help clarify the idea. People who notice will be there in the blink of an eye with you, appreciating the Hygge you help present. Those who won't appreciate it, notwithstanding; in any case, the night will be Hygge.

Great Hygge gatherings

On the off chance that the mindset is correct, Hygge will regularly penetrate all the hot social affairs of the family and spouses. By the time the gatherings of individuals take place after some time of not seeing each other, there is a spell present that is Hygge verifiable. All in all, while you're digging into Hygge's deeper layers, there's no motivation behind why you expand the vibe during most of your big social occasions, especially if you're the one facilitating them.

In case you have the family home for Christmas, a farewell reunion, a birthday or any other occasion, you can increase Hygge's joys throughout the event. Organize your home in the light of the Hygge by playing soothing melodies and extending the atmosphere by candlelight. You will most likely have a quick deal, however this time around; consider making the occasion more and more focused on social collaboration. Set things up with the goal that nurturing is happiness, something to go to in between discussions. A buffet is a great way to do this; your visitors can eat at their own pace and their proposals will not be stopped by the food served.

There is no uncertainty that you have current plans to rely on when engaging visitors and these dishes likely have as many possibilities for Hygge as others. However, in the spirit of Hygge, it never hurts to try something new. While you're done with your friends and family, why not raise the mood by informing everyone of what you realize about Hygge? Either way, getting them to articulate it right will deserve a chuckle. Beyond that, it will be excited to raise the idea you are trying to represent is available while staying with you, developing as others bring their considerations to it.

Try to be an elevated and challenging specialist at work. During the discussion, raise the business goals that you could impart to your co-workers. Likewise, since you're excited about the open doors your business has offered you, check if your co-workers think the same way. Being hyggeligt in the workplace means being the gentleman, positive and warm as much as possible with the people around you. It doesn't hurt if nothing else; you will find that your co-workers float closer and closer to you as they begin to feel the benefits of Hygge without knowing it. A decent way to start this is to show gratitude to your colleagues. The best approach to doing this privilege is to feel that gratitude for them and recognize them as a great motivator. After all, they are your companions for no less than 1/3 of your day. The work environment is his form of life; his imaginable support from the joint efforts of you and your collaborators. When it runs smoothly, you can add something to your overall environment by supporting your needs and the needs of your family. Be aware of the facility you are trying to help and understand that it is handling a direct result of the collaboration between you and the people you work with. When they make your business easier, you can do the same for them by offering a simple "thank you" once in a while. Be aware of the facility you are trying to help and understand that it is handling a direct result of the collaboration between you and the people you work with. When they make your business easier, you can do the same for them by offering a simple "thank you" once in a while.

A little appreciation is extraordinary for bringing this show to the road. From then on, you can focus on different ways your work environment can be transformed into a solid social space. In the long run you can propose extracurricular exercises; intermittent staff parties, possibly an annual pool. Before that, impact your collaborators by setting up a template; consider Hygge during your connections and they will soon start doing the same.

Why are the Danes happy with their relationships?

The Danes know a few things about being happy. Likewise, they know a few things about being happily married. This bliss and happiness is expected in a huge part of the Danish Hygge membership, an unpronounceable word from the American language that sounds dubious like whoogah and includes the desire to make a sound as if it wants to speak. It implies a guarantee of benevolence, comfort, satisfaction and substantial happiness in life. It is about living well, living happy and living with really well-structured seats. At its core, Hygge is about intentionally making a good life and when reaching out to marriage, deliberately making a progressively satisfied and fulfilled association.

Here are just a few of the main reasons Danes can be so much happier with their relationships than other companies on the globe.

Chapter 9: Hygge's impact on the individual, society and the world

So far we have seen the impact of Hygge on the individual and on an entire society. Since society is made up of individuals, if Hygge can increase an individual's happiness and most people in a given society practice Hygge, it could be assumed that a particular society would become happier in general. We have also seen how Hygge can affect other aspects of society as well, including financial stability, environmental well-being, and a whole host of other critical measures. Therefore, it is beyond question that Hygge can have a real impact on both an individual and collective level. The only question to answer is how far the effects of Hygge can go. If Hygge can improve the life of a person and a society, can it also improve the life of the world as a whole? Can Hygge provide the answers humanity so desperately needs at this vital moment in human history? Based on what we have discovered so far, the answer to this question is undoubtedly a resounding "yes". After all, just as society is composed of a large number of individuals, so too the world is composed of a large number of societies. Therefore, if the impact of Hygge on the individual can affect society, the impact of Hygge on society should be able to affect the world.

That influence may be just what humanity needs to restore peace and prosperity to a suffering world in turmoil.

To understand the changes Hygge could bring to the world, it is important to first understand the problems the world is currently struggling with. If you were to ask the average person what would change about the world if he had a magic wand, it would very likely eliminate the constant state of war that parts of the world always seem to be in. It is as if almost every corner of the world is involved in a conflict of one dimension or another. This is the antithesis of the environment that Hygge can create. Just as Hygge can help a single person remove stress and anxiety from their life, and thus live a life of inner and outer peace, so too Hygge could remove much of the hatred and conflicts that drive nations and factions to go to war with each other first. After all, one of the main aspects of Hygge is the pursuit of pleasure. When an individual seeks happy moments, he not only finds happiness and thus relieves stress, but his outlook on life in general also changes.

Rather than looking for reasons to complain or to start arguing, a person who practices Hygge will look for opportunities to be happy. Anyone who tries to be happy will be far less likely to engage a conflict of any kind. When you multiply it to the level of the world collective, that would mean that countries would spend their time and energy finding pleasure rather than trying to dominate and control the rest of the planet. Any country that spent its resources looking for ways in which its entire population could feel comfortable and happy would oppose anything that stands in the way of that ideal. Since war and conflict would undermine the happiness (and fun) that people in a country might experience, it makes sense that a country that practices Hygge strongly avoids anything that would lead to war or conflict.

A very real correlation can easily be drawn between warfare and a nation's overall goal, particularly its cultural value system. Throughout history, it is a common theme that nations that were fixated on depriving themselves of worldly pleasures were far more likely to engage in global conflict of one form or another. Sometimes this conflict took the form of a real war with another developed nation, such as the wars between

Britain and France, or between Britain and Spain, while at other times this conflict took the form of wars of conquest, such as conquest. This trend can also be seen in more recent times, such as in the 20th century with the Second World War. When you examine the cultural values of both Germany and Japan, see the common thread of leaving behind a certain level of worldly pleasure for devotion to duty and service to the state. The idea was not to find happiness in life, but rather to promote nationalism and racial supremacy. This fixation on national identity, particularly as superior to other nations and races, has given rise to the justification for fighting wars of conquest and submission over the seemingly inferior peoples of Earth. Rather than being an isolated incident, this direct relationship between sacrifice and violence can be seen throughout human history.

Conversely, when you look at nations that are focused on finding pleasure and joy in life, you find cultures far less willing to engage in a war of any kind. No wonder the Scandinavian countries, particularly Denmark, have been off the radar in terms of global conflicts for a considerable period. While some might argue that Denmark's size is what prevents them from being a global threat, it would be worth pointing out that Britain, the Netherlands and even Japan are not very different in size, yet all of these countries do have been involved in global conflicts for the past few centuries. When it comes to war, a simple rule of thumb prevails: "Where there is a will, there is none." The size of a nation does not necessarily determine whether or not that nation will be able to wage war on another nation in the world. Rather, it is determined by the heart of a nation. Therefore, countries that focus on the pursuit of happiness and peace in everyday life, regardless of size, are the ones that will avoid conflict at virtually all costs. It is the prime example of a nation that embraces peace and happiness. They are the ones who will avoid conflict at practically all costs. Denmark is a good example. Its current status as the seat of the Hygge, just as Tibet is the seat of Buddhism, means that the nation as a whole has no interest in causing harm or suffering, neither to its people nor to other people in the world in general.

Just to bring the point home in a way that might be easier to measure, consider the fact that Denmark was one of the home countries of the infamous Vikings, who engaged in global wars of various forms several centuries ago.

Viking culture is also what helps create Hygge culture shows just how meaningful the Hygge lifestyle is. After all, Denmark is a modern beacon of happiness and peace, a far cry from their 9th-century reputation. Now, instead of being the nation of merciless and bloodthirsty warriors wielding swords and axes, Denmark is a nation of happiness, pleasure and a sense of general well-being. That this definition comes simultaneously with the rise in popularity of the Hygge tradition is no mere coincidence. Rather, it demonstrates the real correlation between Hygge and the national identity of 21st century Denmark. Imagine, if a country can reinvent itself thanks to Hygge, how different could the world be if every country did the same?

In addition to potentially ending any kind of armed conflict, Hygge could help eliminate various other threats to the world at large. One of these threats is the destruction of the environment. Although there are several reasons why the planet is facing environmental challenges of different forms, the exploitation of minerals and other natural resources by man is perhaps the most significant. It is certainly the most controllable and the one that would be directly impacted if the world as a whole started practicing Hygge. Since Hygge reduces the influence of materialism and consumerism, it makes sense that if the world followed a lifestyle in step with Hygge, the need to extract minerals and raw materials would drop exponentially. Furthermore, excess waste that is dumped in landfills would be reduced, resulting in environmental protection "at both ends" so to speak. Not only would the environment not be depleted of resources it would also not be turned into a landfill for humanity's waste. Unfortunately, as many countries remain rooted in hyper-consumerism, it seems the environment is far from being cared for in the way it deserves and needs. However, you just have to look to countries like Denmark, where consumerism is not the way of life, to see how the environment could be improved if more than the world adopted the Hygge lifestyle. It seems that the environment is very far from being cared for in the way it deserves and needs.

Another way the environment would benefit from Hygge is that humanity would stop treating it as unimportant. The number one reason why so many industries continue to dump waste and toxic materials into rivers and oceans is that they have simply lost all sense of respect and admiration for nature. Because Hygge promotes spending time in nature to find peace and happiness, it ultimately promotes a greater love and appreciation for nature. The result is a more symbiotic relationship between man and the environment. When this relationship is restored, the abuses against nature and the environment end. No person or entity who truly appreciated nature would continue to poison rivers and oceans with waste material. Furthermore, the need for oil and gas would decline exponentially as more and more people begin to use less intrusive forms of transport than those requiring fossil fuels. This would not only help protect the environment from continued drilling and mining, but it would also help clear the air of carbon gases that are beginning to cause all sorts of environmental problems. If more people around the world respected and protected nature, as is part of the Hygge lifestyle, then it is possible that this threat can be stopped before it is too late but it would also help to clean the air from the carbon gases that are starting to cause all sorts of environmental problems. Whether or not you accept the science, the fact is that climate change is a real threat to this planet.

Finally, there's the impact Hygge could have on things like famine, disease, and other similar dangers that threaten the lives of millions of people. While Hygge isn't necessarily rooted in helping other people, it does help foster a greater sense of community. This is especially true in terms of family. By spending more time with family and friends, a person can hardly turn a blind eye when members of their inner circle are struggling in life. It makes sense that as your friends and family become more important to you, you would want to help them whenever possible. Again, this isn't necessarily a direct purpose of Hygge, but it is a very real side effect of practicing a Hygge lifestyle. If this attitude were taken globally, therefore nations around the world would make a greater effort to assist in places affected by famine, disease and natural disasters. Instead of making a symbolic effort for the sake of appearance, countries would strive to solve problems and bring lasting relief to those affected. This would be a global manifestation of the Hygge sense of family and community. By embracing each nation as part of the global family, no country would be able to stand by while the population of another nation suffered and died. Furthermore, as consumerism and greed are replaced by generosity and gratitude through Hygge, it makes sense for leaders and citizens of every nation to find joy in such endeavors. Instead of using humanitarian efforts to exert political leverage, nations would use them to increase the happiness and fulfillment of all concerned. All in all, Hygge could transform the world into a place where humanity respects nature, preserves peace and promotes happiness and well-being to all life and people on planet Earth.

Chapter 10: The Danish method of educating children for happiness

Before delving into the Danish method, let's start with a fundamental premise. The dream of all mothers is to see their baby happy, but:

- Can you educate to serenity?

- Can you be taught to be people who were formed in the name of happiness?

- Is there an educational and behavioral system to face life and the stages of childhood with this positivity?

The Danish method is not simply an educational system to be applied at school, but a behavioral approach to permeate the social and daily fabric of children and their parents. A path to live satisfied and raise happy children.

Educating children about happiness in school and life

What makes our children happy? I want to start from an episode of my childhood that took place within the walls of the school to reflect on the suggestions that derive from the Danish method. In elementary school I had a math teacher who made me hate the subject, in the sense that I was convinced I didn't have the neurons to understand it! The checks were conducted by having us put real barricades around the benches, so as not to copy. He was only allowed to go down the hall after his class test. All this has acted on the sense of competition (with the "let's see who comes first" effect) and has certainly not fueled mutual support and help. I was terrified of that approach and for five years I never went down the hall. The discomfort generated was never expressed to the teacher.

Listening to the empathic soul was completely absent

Here, this pedagogical method is opposed to the Danish one, summarized with the acronym PARENT to underline how decisive is the role and the peaceful and relaxed attitude of parents. The school is just one of the many environments in which the educational system can be applied, which embraces all phases of daily life, therefore also family, friends and society. The school teaching given by the knowledge of the subjects is not the only relevant element and is accompanied by the development of other specific skills of the child.

Live happily with the game

At this point, you are wondering what the secret of happiness is. The key is playable for free. Through this activity the child is trained, vented, learns to manage the various tests and to face his fears. Play is one of the inspiring principles of the Danish PARENT method which translates into:
- ✓ Play;
- ✓ No ultimatum;
- ✓ Authenticity;
- ✓ Reframing;
- ✓ Empathy;
- ✓ Solidarity.

How much do we influence our children with the choices we make?

As a parent, I wonder what my attitude is and the choices I make for my child. I've been wondering since my pregnancy. I wonder how much my reactions can affect, inhibit, hinder or encourage a child's growth.

The message that I "take-home" from Jessica Joelle Alexander's book is contained in four macro-areas: I find them useful tips that are good for moms, dads and babies.

Confidence

The key concept is achieved through self-esteem. The latter, as already mentioned, is determined by free play, by the possibility of experimenting, trying, testing. Children breathe our anxiety, so we try to remove what frightens us, the dangers are often our problems and not theirs. This way we avoid passing on negative feelings to children. Undoubtedly useful to assign children tasks such as tidying a room or setting the table, this encourages them to respect the place where they are. One point that got me thinking is the "awards ceremony". What attitudes should be rewarded? Instead of praising them for the vows they take, it is more constructive to recognize the value of the kindness and cooperation that these gestures show and gratify.

Empathy

How to create a good climate in which children can experiment? Thanks to empathy we lay the foundations for a healthy environment, where no one is judged, but only seen, taken into consideration, listened to and involved to naturally nurture a sense of belonging. I take a cue from my bad and traumatic experience as an elementary school girl to emphasize how important it is to learn to read yourself and others, listen to your feelings and feelings. Once again, thanks to an empathic fabric in which adults raise children, emotional honesty is transmitted, not the pursuit of perfection.

Sincerity

This aspect intervenes in an incisive way on the climate of serenity. It means letting children know the truth about everything. Even on topics often considered uncomfortable such as death or sex. This pushes you to become more aware, helps you grow resilient and peaceful and somehow more in tune with your person. Here the ability of adults to relate to their children without taboos takes care of communication. Discover tips for raising a child who talks to parents.

Courage

In the Danish method, the courage to make mistakes is trained without being afraid of judgment. The attitude of trying, taking risks, experimenting and getting back on the game is always cultivated. In this way, we allow ourselves the opportunity to learn from our mistakes and grow strong. The nature of this constructive approach is undoubtedly exciting and leads to success in terms of the quality of the path followed and not as a synonym for perfection. The proposed lifestyle leads to the growth of happy children, nourishes their involvement in the community by feeling an active part and consequently facilitating the progressive reduction of bullying.

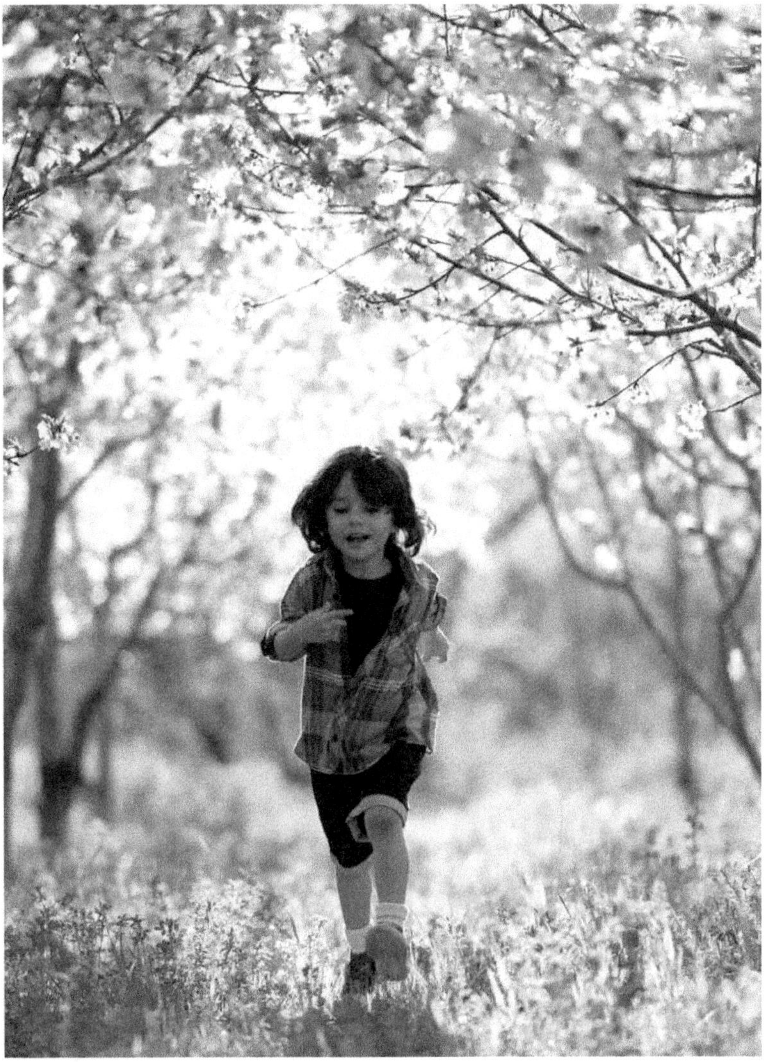

Chapter 11: How to apply Hygge realistically if you have an avoidable lifestyle

A key tenant of Danish culture for decades, Hygge has recently taken the wider world by storm. This is partly due to the design's steadily increasing popularity, but also because it highlights savoring the moment in a crowded world of unlimited Instagram posts along with a never-ending cycle of news.

However, Hygge isn't something we can easily define as it doesn't just refer to the number of candles you've packed on the mantel. Hygge means bringing all the people you love together in one room to make you feel warm at home; it's about eating spicy food that scares you, and it's about creating an oasis in a gloomy climate. So even if your lifestyle may be too active to allow for lazy nights on the couch, here's our guide on how to get your Hygge fix, wherever you are.

Adopt the light

To give your distance that tranquil Hygge vibe, focus on creating the best lighting. Make the most of natural light whenever possible by lifting the blinds, sitting by a window to bask in its beautiful light. Since Denmark has long, dark winters, artificial lighting has been integrated, through ceiling fixtures and fragrance-free candles.

Community

Community plays a vital role in Hygge, as it is believed that the comforts of life are increased in the company of friends. You can apply it to any range of actions: from watching a movie and sipping coffee by the fire or hiking in the woods to just reading a book next to someone else.

Savor the flavors

Hygge involves all five senses, so food shouldn't be overlooked. Hot drinks like coffee, tea, and glögg (Scandinavian mulled wine) and hearty dishes like cake, pastries, and porridge can help you get the greatest Hygge. Plus, it ties in with the concept of community: food and drink taste better when loved by loved ones too!

Hygge at work

Most companies will ban candles burning in the office (as it's a fairly obvious fire hazard) but they might be fine with using a slim infuser. Smell is intrinsically connected to mood, so adorable White Company speakers could be the difference between a great day and a terrible day. Another essential aspect of Hygge is maintaining heat, keeping a hot water bottle on the table is great for beating the cold in the workplace. Finally, even the evilest companies allow you to keep your people closest and dearest, so take advantage of that and invest in frames that can do your favorite photos justice.

Hygge in the gym

With all this talk of coziness and pampering, it's easy to believe that Hygge is a lazy person. However, exercise is very Hygge - it's about producing heat, feeling the best you can feel, even physically, and maximizing your potential for self-indulgence.

Wearing gym clothing that you feel comfortable in is key, and if you're an outdoor runner, a sports vest may be your best bet this season. Above all, exercise is meant to make you feel good, so be sure to reward yourself after hitting the gym!

Hygge's feel is warm and comfortable. It is how we feel if we are hot while there is a thunderstorm outside or the sensation of a hot cup in our palms. Laugh with family and friends by candlelight along with the gratification of a stomach full of fantastic food and drink. It's easy to see why this kind of lifestyle attitude is really meaningful to this Dane. Denmark has a harsh and cold climate, but still has good all-natural beauty. Having the ability to associate with this environment while maintaining relaxation is exactly what Hygge is all about.

What's so amazing about Hygge is that it's something we can all incorporate into our daily life. It's about taking the time to delight in the things, people and places you love, whether that means taking some time out during your lunch break to take a walk or finish the day with a warm cup of tea and a novel instead of scrolling endlessly via Instagram. We can all afford multiple times like these today. In today's civilization, achievement and hard work often take priority, and as significant as these elements are, it's easy to forget that people should also take the time to relax and enjoy the present. After all, that's why we've worked so hard.

Creating Hygge: implementing the moment

Hygge means realizing where you are and taking some time to connect to yourself! Do you want a quiet moment on your own? Do you want to be with the people you adore? What do you want?

Once you understand, find the quietest and easiest way to satisfy these desires. For example, if I want a minute alone, I make my favorite tea, then curl up in bed and listen to my favorite audiobook. Do you want to spend time with friends? Have a game night or even a potluck!

A significant and typically unspoken aspect of Hygge is to disconnect. Stay away from your phone and remember that watching TV is a relaxation method and not a requirement. Hygge means being present in the moment and being indulgent with yourself, including rest from what you are doing.

Creating Hygge: components for a Hygge day

While it's important to integrate Hygge into the simpler parts of the day (for example, wearing your favorite sweater or flannel), pajamas are the easiest items to use to get into your comfort zone. Maybe you're more of an oversized t-shirt and sweatpants, rather than a matching set of tops and bottoms, but this collection is still nice to have (as intentionality and focus have amazing capabilities).

The rest of the equation is just creating your comfort. Find your favorite blanket and mug (the warmer, the better) and give yourself a gentle atmosphere through fairy lights or candlelight.

1. Take some time to take a break and relax a couple of times a day: once in the afternoon, once in the late day and at night. During breaks, do not send text messages, use other technologies, or watch TV.

2. Do a very simple meditation a few times a day, preferably in the evening and in the morning. If you can do it during the day too, so much the better. Meditation doesn't have to be complex. It can be as simple as sitting in a comfortable chair, taking a couple of deep breaths, setting a timer for about ten minutes, then closing your eyes and focusing on your breath. After the buzzer goes off signaling the end of time, open your eyes and take a couple of minutes to hear how good it feels to be relaxed. So you can resume your normal activities with greater clarity and focus.

3. Live in the moment as much as possible. Try not to think too much about scenarios or parts of your daily life. Instead, try to pay attention to your breathing a couple of times a day. Take the opportunity to enjoy the view wherever you are. There is always something extraordinary around us and all we have to do is see it.

4. Try spending some time outside. This could be a short walk in the park or just going out at lunchtime and looking for a quiet, green spot. This will revive your energy and allow you to feel much more relaxed and closer to nature. Plus, it could ground you and help you reside in the moment, indifferent to the future or the past.

By taking these measures, you will get greater satisfaction. This could make you feel much fitter and happier. When the weekend comes, you can practice many of those tactics. They will bring balance to your life and restore your energy.

Chapter 12: Improve performance and job satisfaction through Hygge

The practice of Hygge goes beyond the home and yourself. It can also be used to improve the work environment to promote employee collaboration, productivity and well-being.

How is it possible?

As explained earlier, Hygge isn't just about buying associated things or organizing the office in a certain way. You don't see a hyggeligt workplace, but rather you feel it day after day. As such, it makes people want to go to work every single day. The reason they work is not just to earn money, but also because they enjoy what they are doing.

When job satisfaction is high, there is an atmosphere conducive to achieving the following:

- **Employee welfare**

Several organizations considered leaders in their respective fields recognize the value of ensuring the well-being of their employees. In addition to preventing them from being overly fatigued and vulnerable to illness, improving employee well-being contributes to their ability to produce more creative and innovative results. Furthermore, studies show that placing a high value on well-being allows the organization to retain its employees for a longer period and dissuades them from thinking of leaving the organization for a competitor.

In light of these benefits, many companies today are looking for ways to understand how to promote the well-being of their employees. Experts point them to various strategies, one of which is the concept of Hygge.

- **Physical well-being**

Workspace design experts recommend setting up seats and desks that allow for various types of posture. Requiring employees to simply sit down while they work can be particularly damaging to their health. As such, the workplace must include furniture that can also be used while standing or lying down. This is where Hygge comes in. It promotes the idea of using soft sofas, soft armchairs and cozy mattresses, which employees can use depending on the type of work they are doing. Some companies refrain from assigning dedicated workstations to each employee so that anyone can choose the place that would make them feel more comfortable and focused.

For those who prefer to stand upright, desks that can be adjusted accordingly are also highly encouraged. Rather than metal or plastic desks, Hygge encourages the use of wooden desks for a more authentic vibe that also elevates the aesthetics of the workplace.

Letting in natural light from outside not only benefits businesses by contributing to energy savings, but also reduces employee stress levels, making them feel more energetic throughout the day.

Pantry areas allow employees to socialize while having meals together. Hygge preaches the value of eating with other people, not only because he wants you to be more sociable, but also because eating together could lead to the adoption of healthier eating habits exhibited by those around you.

Some employers offer special benefits to their employees. These are not the kind of benefits that are not required by law nor are they commonly granted by many companies. Popular examples of such perks include free on-site massages and comfortable sleeping capsules.

- **Cognitive well-being**

A hyggeligt workspace improves employees' ability to focus on their work, while also offering them spaces to rest and rejuvenate at some point during the workday. Organizations create these kinds of workspaces:

1. Place live plants in different parts of the office

Hygge wants you to create a strong bond with nature, but it can be difficult when you have to work most of the day. Some organizations offer their employees this opportunity by taking inspiration from nature for their interior decoration.

This doesn't mean you have to spend thousands of dollars just to green your office. One of the simplest and most hyggeligt ways to do this is to set up parts of the workplace dedicated to living plants. Depending on the level of commitment and the available space that can be allocated, this can be done by creating a mini garden somewhere on the premises or by arranging potted plants around the office.

Both methods work effectively in producing the desired positive effect on employee mental well-being. The sight of natural greens could help relieve stress and tension, as well as fatigue.

Studies also show that workspaces that house establishments tend to have employees with greater ability to focus on their respective tasks for an extended period.

2. Playing music in the background

Employees, particularly those working on a production line, may be able to produce ever-increasing quality output when the right kind of melody is played in the background. Music helps them get into the ideal rhythm that is best suited to their type of work.

Music can be extremely hyggeligt when it inspires positive feelings among those who listen to it. In addition to increasing productivity, certain types of music can calm a stressed individual or provide the right atmosphere to relax the body and mind.

Given the benefits of music, a growing number of companies are looking at how to best leverage the hyggeligt qualities of music for the betterment of their employees.

3. Apply the ideal palette to improve cognitive performance in the office interior

The psychology of color emphasizes the propensity of the human mind to be significantly influenced by colors. Studies show that with the right set of colors, an employee's job quality, productivity and overall mood can be greatly improved.

Hygge isn't associated with a specific color, but it encourages you to get in touch with nature. Therefore, the best way to take advantage of both color psychology and Hygge is to apply colors that can be found in nature to the workspace.

For reference, here are the suggested hyggeligt colors and their respective effects on work performance:

- **Blue**

  - Calm the mind;
  - Lower your heart rate and blood pressure;
  - It fosters communication and trust.

Given these effects, blue is best applied for areas used for brainstorming with the team.

- **Yellow**

- Promotes optimistic feelings and mindsets;
- Provides an energy boost;
- Stimulates the mind to think.

Due to such effects, you should consider using yellow only as an accent as too much can agitate the temperament and anxiety of employees. However, if you intend to make it the main color, apply it for workspaces used to come up with creative and innovative ideas.

- **Green**

- Increase creativity;
- Inspire innovative thinking;
- Reduces anxiety;
- Prevents eye fatigue;
- Promotes balance and harmony.

Since green has powerful yet calming effects, it is best applied for offices that rely primarily on computers for daily operations.

- White

- Makes the workspace spacious;
- Increase creativity.

The blank slate that white gifts stimulate the mind to come up with creative ideas. Hence, it is best used for areas where employees create plans and projects.

• Emotional well-being

In addition to ensuring the physical and mental well-being of employees, it is also important and beneficial, in the long term, to take care of their emotional stability. This way, they would be able to feel more comfortable with their superiors, teammates, and subordinates.

There are various ways to ensure the emotional well-being of employees.

Here are the best tips you should consider doing at work:

- **Spend your lunch break outdoors**

Some employees feel compelled to have lunch at their workstations so they can stay on top to receive important emails when they arrive, or so they can plan their next projects. Having this type of habit can be abrasive not only to your cognitive performance but also to your emotional well-being.

Studies show that employees who do this tend to have increased stress levels, thereby decreasing their control over their emotions and their ability to handle difficult situations throughout the day. Since they haven't had time to recharge properly, their job performance suffers despite their intention to be more productive at work.

To avoid making the same mistake, you should practice the hyggeligt way of eating your lunch during a workday. Since you are unlikely to go home and have lunch with your family, the next best option is to go out and have lunch alone or with your colleagues.

You can go to the nearest cafe and buy a nice sandwich and a glass of fresh fruit juice for lunch. If you prefer to prepare and pack your food, take it with you to the nearest park and eat it there.

When you are out, remember to relax both your body and mind. Breathe in some fresh air. If the weather is pleasant, appreciate the sensation of sunlight on your skin. Forget the activities you need to work on when you come back from break Focus on the moment and enjoy your time away from your desk.

- **Personalize your desk or workstation**

Most people spend most of their day in the office, so it's best to turn it into something that feels like home. Offices nowadays are more forgiving when it comes to decorating their employees' workspaces.

Unless you work in a manufacturing company or workshop, you will likely enjoy a greater degree of freedom when it comes to carrying some personal items that can be used to decorate your workspace. If you haven't thought about doing it yet, here are some good ideas you could try on your own:

- Framed pictures of your family and friends;
- Memorable holiday souvenirs;
- A collection of different tea leaves stored in a beautiful wooden box;

- Scented candles, if permitted by the company;

- A bouquet of your favorite flowers placed in a vase;

- A work of art made by you, a family member or friend.

Using such items to upgrade your desk or workstation can make you feel more comfortable at work. When you are stressed out, you can just look at them and reflect on their meaning or memories attached to them. Eventually, you will feel calmer and more energetic again, ready to take on the rest of your workday.

- **Give employees sincere recognition**

As explained earlier, Hygge isn't just about turning your workplace into a cozy place or spending your lunch break with your colleagues. It's also about creating a workplace where employees feel valued.

Expressing sincerity by encouraging words and gestures helps reduce stress levels and raise employee morale. Such kindness also increases their resilience, allowing them to move forward even in the face of various challenges during the working day.

Once a culture of sincere recognition is established, employees themselves would gradually help it grow and spread in the workplace. Performing random acts of kindness as a way to repay him would become more common every day. As a result, Hygge can be felt and experienced by everyone and everywhere within the workplace.

Collaboration between employees

Hygge supports employee collaboration by promoting activities and set-ups that encourage openness, kindness and communication. Traditional means of achieving this, such as conducting daily briefings and assigning employees to group projects, could only work at a certain level. Bringing them closer to each other on a much deeper level requires applying the principles of hyggeligt in the daily operations of the company.

Below are some great ideas that your HR specialists would agree with:

- **Organize or participate in team building activities**

Embracing the spirit of teamwork is a key step in achieving a hyggeligt workspace. Therefore, employers should attach importance to exercises that enhance employees' sense of belonging to each other.

However, team-building activities take time to plan and execute.

- **Water sports activities**

Most companies include going to the beach as one of their planned team building activities. This in itself is hyggeligt as it allows employees to spend time together while enjoying the sun, sand and waves. To elevate it even further, however, you should also consider doing water sports in the itinerary.

It doesn't have to be as extreme as jet skiing or surfing, nor does it have to be kept only on beaches. If there's a river or lake nearby, head there for a day of canoeing, kayaking, or even sport fishing. These activities promote collaboration between employees by bringing them even closer to nature.

• Karaoke Nights

Several companies find this to be one of the simplest yet fun ways to foster camaraderie among employees. It's easy enough to organize a karaoke night these days because you can simply make a reservation at a karaoke bar or set it up yourself with a smart TV, speakers, and microphones.

Through the karaoke nights, employees would have a chance to relax and have fun while discovering the hidden talents of their colleagues. Plus, song choices are excellent conversation sources, especially when you find others who have the same taste in music as you.

• Room escape challenges

Room escape games have become more popular in recent years. However, they're not just for recreational fun with your family and friends. Human resources specialists have recognized this type of business as an excellent way to hone employee leadership skills, patience, creative thinking and teamwork.

If you're not familiar with this, a room escape challenge involves locking a group of people inside a room for a set period. Within that limit, the group must find clues and solve puzzles to break free.

Without strong collaboration between participants, this activity could be particularly difficult or even impossible to do. Therefore, including room escape challenges in annual teambuilding plans is highly recommended for any organization.

- **Volunteering for local institutions**

For an even more advantageous use of time, team building activities can be combined with volunteer work. The latter is generally classified only under the corporate social responsibility (CSR) of the company. However, inviting employees to take part in this could inspire them to better connect with each other while caring for those in need.

Common examples of volunteer work that can be turned into a team-building exercise include:

- Feeding the homeless during the holidays;

- Provide on-site assistance to institutions for people with special needs;

- Distribution of gifts in a children's hospital.

Involving your employees in the company's CSR activities also increases the success of these initiatives. Studies also show that these activities improve the emotional well-being of employees when conducted regularly.

• Invite your colleagues to a potluck party at your home

Good food eaten alongside other people exemplifies some of the best values associated with Hygge. Since this type of lifestyle also promotes the idea of a frugal life, you could save money by organizing a potluck dinner for your coworkers rather than hanging out with them in restaurants or bars.

A potluck differs from a regular dinner party due to this important requirement: each attendee must contribute at least one dish, typically home-cooked, which can be shared among all party attendees.

Instead of just one or two people in charge of the food, everyone can prepare something special that they want others to enjoy too.

Conversations at a potluck party could also be a lot more interesting because you may find out who among your colleagues has hidden talents when it comes to cooking or baking. Also, people usually make something special for potlucks, such as recipes that have been passed on within families. Bringing these themes to dinner allows everyone to know each other better, thus fostering deeper and stronger bonds that are essential for more effective collaborations at work.

• Create shared workspaces for employees

Open layouts don't just apply to homes. Offices can also benefit greatly from reducing closed offices and using cubicles.

To give employees even more opportunity to collaborate, place tables and chairs around the office that can accommodate at least four people. This way they will have spaces that can be used for group work and brainstorming sessions. It facilitates the flow of ideas by providing them with drawing boards and portable markers, as well as projectors or screens.

Hygge was originally developed by the Danish people to combat the harsh conditions they experience during the winter. Nowadays, it is no longer limited to just cold and dark nights. Its scope continues to expand as people continually discover ways to introduce Hygge into different aspects of life, including the workplace.

Happiness, comfort, and safety may not be the first things you think about when you're asked what are the best ways to increase employee productivity and creativity. However, as demonstrated by the Danes and various studies conducted on the effects of working in a hyggeligt workplace, it has been shown that bringing the comforts and familiarity of a home to the workplace ensures the general well-being of employees and improves the way people work. These two points significantly contribute to employee job satisfaction, which is considered to be one of the key factors that make the company's performance and profitability to even greater levels.

Chapter 13: Practical Hygge

Happiness is a warm and fragrant corner within the walls of the home. Hygge is the Scandinavian way of living happily. Here's how to apply it to your home to make it warm, welcoming and comfortable. The key to living better and longer is scientifically proven: a warm and welcoming home that causes us to slow down and relax puts us at ease and makes us happy because we are content with simply what we have.

Therefore, the recipe for happiness exists and it takes little to implement it and experience its benefits in person. A cup of coffee in the morning, a lunch in the living room, a book read on the sofa near the crackling fire, a hot bath at the end of the day: Hygge is all this and the feeling of well-being to be shared in harmony with relatives, family and friends in different environments obviously adequate. And considering that this trend is no longer a Danish prerogative, why not take advantage of the coziness and warmth of the home during the winter to make it more welcoming and comfortable all year round?

Well thought out spaces and banished disorder. A first step in embracing the Hygge philosophy is to be aware of the spaces by letting them talk about you and take care of the house. Consider what you have and what you can add and change to make it more welcoming, instill this awareness in all members of your family, including children, and try to invest in smart solutions to contain the disorder and store what you don't use frequently. Remember that the Hygge space is also silent and harmonious, also and above all in the colors. Living in a Hygge way means making the home a meeting place, for a stress-free exchange of opinions, ideas in a relaxed way, meeting friends and family in a peaceful oasis environment. And in particular, the Hyggekrog is a part of the house where you can spend time in a hyggeligt way.

10 things make the house more hyggeligt:

- Place in the house, usually in the living room, where you can sit between the cushions with a blanket;
- Chimney;
- Candles;
- Wooden objects;
- Nature;
- Books;
- Ceramic objects;
- Coverings of different invoices;
- Vintage furniture;

- Pillows and blankets.

A personal corner

Fundamental for the psychological well-being of the human being is the possibility of having a personal place that functions as a welcoming refuge when living in one's home. As children, we experience it and ask for it without filters: a room all to ourselves, where we can give life to our world. As an adult, it can be more difficult to defend your space but you need to do it. Create a corner of the house that is yours alone: an armchair with your favorite plaid on it, a table with your magazines and books, your teapot. Imagine being there when you are out and about to go home.

The ideal temperature

There is nothing cozier than a warm home in the winter. A good boiler can be a perfect investment (choose one with an extended warranty for peace of mind). Always use it with awareness and moderation: you have to manage the internal temperature so that it is warmer and more enveloping in winter, but never dry. Improve the air quality in your home by using essential oils and humidifiers to spread a good, revitalizing and comforting aroma in all environments.

Design and order

Everything in its place and a place for everything: a tidy and clean home environment makes you happier. Spend a day cleaning up your home environment with the space cleaning technique. Throwing away (or putting in the attic) is often the best cure for the stress of the clutter that crowds our lives. Then reward yourself by purchasing a design object you have long wanted: lamp, coffee table, desk furniture or that electric kettle you never bought.

A quality bed (also aesthetic)

The quality of sleep affects our life and our daily happiness, but having a good mattress is not enough. How is your bed? Look at it and give it a frank score: it must entice you to spend a comfortable night and a few mornings in total laziness. If not, invest in a new pair of sheets (crumpled linen sheets that don't iron are very practical) and a good number of decorative pillows. A plaid to wear in contrasting colors helps to make everything even more comfortable.

Hygge style bedroom

In the bedroom, the choice of furniture is focused on the search for the bare minimum, without unnecessary frills. Enjoying life with a few simple things means having ample space in the bedroom, so go ahead for small wooden wardrobes, needing a few essentials while a bed edge rug will make getting into bed warm.

Hygge style lounge

Focusing on creating a relaxing environment in the living room is imperative for those who choose this style. It is, in fact, the meeting place and relaxation par excellence, and it must be made as soft and comfortable as possible with sofas, cushions, seats, to facilitate being at ease. A large dense and soft pile rug, on which to lie down cuddling with large cushions, useful as seats and to support the neck and back while, in the winter seasons, blankets and woolen plaids allow you to stay warm if there is no fireplace in the living room, a traditional element in Danish homes. There is no shortage of sofas and armchairs, especially in the models with chaise longue that allow you to relax, rest to rest or read a good book in front of the fireplace.

Hygge style bathroom

The place to relax and dedicate yourself to body care. The only room in the apartment where you are used to being alone, furnishing and equipping the bathroom in a soft and relaxing way is not complicated in itself. Compared to the more practical shower, the tub is ideal, being able to soak for a long time without any rush. Small accessories such as a wall mirror and a ladder for storing towels and bathrobes will be more than enough for the relaxation area.

Hygge, the way to "happy" clothing

To fully experience Hygge you must be dressed in the most comfortable clothes you have: baggy pants, long sweaters, wool socks, soft dresses, a dressing gown and a t-shirt. You don't wear sophisticated clothes to experience Hygge, you don't need anything expensive or designer, Hygge is humble and slow: simplicity. She is watching from the window as the strong wind blows out and covers you with a grandmother's shawl.

How's the Hygge style? But, of course, a casual and easy style! The Nordic style is minimalist, simple in lines, comfortable in materials, mainly natural like wool and cotton. The feeling of well-being is preferred rather than pursuing formal elegance. It is a casual style. The indispensable elements of Hygge:

- Wool scarves, stoles and shawls;
- Knitted sweaters;
- Baggy pants like pajamas or pajamas;
- Wool socks;
- Handmade items - handmade.-

Hygge and me

Hygge for me is not a discovery never tried, on the contrary, it corresponds very much to my lifestyle, the discovery was finding a name that identifies a situation, a feeling and that helps me to live fully and consciously emotions and special moments.

Beauty in the book is finding a series of recipes to recreate it, look for it, bring it into everyday life and thus be truly more grateful and happier.

And after all, what are we looking for if not the happiness and love of sharing with loved ones? Danish women, with their enveloping and soft outfits, have become true style icons to be inspired by for the cold season. Here's what to copy from their wardrobes for a living fashion.

Hygge is a word hard to pronounce, almost impossible to translate...but to be experienced. What is it about? It is not something that can be touched or seen. It is something that, quite simply, can be felt. It is, in fact, a sensation, a warm and safe sensation, a state of profound well-being. It is the basis of the Danish method and is based on the harmony of a community, on happiness cultivated in every moment, on the ability to savor the little things in life.

In Denmark, this particular attitude to well-being and happiness is sought and translated into many aspects of daily life, which thus become tools to feel good and live in full Hygge style. The wardrobe is no exception: it is precisely from this philosophy that Danish women have developed their way of experiencing fashion, thus becoming true style icons, especially in the more casual fashion dedicated to every day. Here are 4 things to absolutely copy from their outfits, to bring some Hygge spirit and a touch of authentic Danish style into your wardrobe.

The Danish palette

The palette to focus on for a perfect Danish style is made up of 50 shades of black, there is no doubt! Black and all shades of gray are the basis of the wardrobes of Danish women, who tend to show off total black or total gray looks with great ease in the most desperate situations. Their secret? Playing with textures and overlapping elements, for a personal effect, never banal or flat.

If you are not a lover of very classic black, however, do not worry: the alternative exists and is made up of natural and neutral colors, such as light beige or white. And the color? It is not banned from the wardrobe but must be dosed with extreme caution and used mainly in stains, for example on small accessories such as hats or scarves.

Hygge inspirations for cooking

It is now fashionable to talk about the Hygge lifestyle, this untranslatable Danish term means living life without stress, enjoying the little things, treating yourself to moments of happiness even through simple gestures, every day like choosing relaxing furniture, filling the house with flowers, spending of time in the middle of nature. This lifestyle also involves the culinary sphere, the act of cooking and sharing a meal are moments to be lived in harmony, seeking pleasure even in gestures that may seem repetitive, it is part of Hygge thinking, for example, put aside the excuse of - I don't know how to cook, I don't have time - to take care of yourself.

Sign up for a cooking class within your reach, not only will you learn new concepts and recipes but it will also be a means to meet new people, socialize, or create a sort of rotating kitchen with friends, colleagues, relatives, useful for not stressful moments and experiences of conviviality. Open up to new flavors, cultures, savor unknown dishes, be curious to experiment with new combinations, try to taste an ingredient that doesn't excite you, enjoy the moment you sit down at the table.

Recipes in full Hygge style, we talk about Danish dishes but of course the ideas are endless, smorrebrod, is buttered bread with avocado, eggs, salmon, shrimps, vegetables, sprouts, cheese, it is usually composed at the moment, a fun moment in which the imagination is stimulated in creating one's own we improperly call it sandwich. The cinnamon rolls, the Danes are used to indulging in a sweet pleasure once a day, rolls but also chocolate, marzipan, cream, butter, a little greedy moment to be fully enjoyed.

Another important role among Hygge dishes, soups, fish, vegetables, spices, legumes, rice, cereals, hot dishes that heat up and can be prepared in many variations; meatballs, usually accompanied by potatoes and presented with gravy, beef, venison, game. The glogg, a hot drink typical of Scandinavian countries, made with wine, spices, sometimes almonds, recalls our mulled wine. No matter what the recipe is, to lead a Hygge lifestyle you just have to prepare it with taste, pleasure, perhaps in company, totally savoring the flavor and comfort it gives you.

What makes Hygge magical is sharing, being together, feeling surrounded by affection like when you are at the table with dear friends. Which foods according to the Danes are most reassuring and can convey this feeling of warmth? We also discover 10 recipes that can help us feel better, especially when temperatures drop dramatically, it's bad weather and the days get shorter.

- **Hot Chocolate**: What could be more reassuring and enjoyable than keeping a cup of hot chocolate sunk in your armchair? Maybe in the same place where your grandfather used to read you storybooks when you were little. All of this is Hygge and can be recreated in minutes. For perfect hot chocolate, mix cocoa powder with milk. Separately, melt a few pieces of dark chocolate. Bring the milk to a boil and add the melted chocolate.

- **Fish soup**: it is a classic of Scandinavian cuisine, a warm pleasure that pampers the stomach and the spirit. It is no coincidence that soup recipes are widespread in all cultures. Based on vegetables, legumes, rice, cereals, spices: so there are many possible variations. Denmark, surrounded on three sides by the sea, could only do with a very common raw material such as fish, the protagonist of this recipe. To this are added carrots, celery, leek and garlic. Finally, the cream that guarantees creaminess and makes a dish of poor origin more substantial.

- **Pea soup** (glue ærter): it is a Danish recipe that has more than 200 years of history. In these centuries it has brought comfort and warmth to thousands and thousands of people, starting from the countryside to the exclusive restaurants of the capital. Many variations develop from the traditional dish, from the simplest to the most refined and sophisticated. The base remains of yellow peas. Traditionally, to add more flavor and substance to the whole, pork is added.

- **Meatballs**: another dish present in different traditions, ready to wrap our taste buds in a soft embrace.
Scandinavian meatballs are of Swedish origin but it doesn't matter, all of this is Hygge. Usually, minced pork, beef or game is used and everything is presented with a thick roast sauce, an element that certainly makes our recipe more succulent. Don't forget the side dish of boiled potatoes, another symbol of Scandinavian cuisine.

- **Cinnamon Rolls**: These are similar to American cinnamon rolls. What is the difference? That the Danish recipe is not filled with dried fruit. What makes these soft sweetbreads special is the intense aroma and flavor of cinnamon. After all, isn't it the aroma that reminds us most of Christmas, the time of year when you feel (or should feel) the warmth of your loved ones the most? Start the day with a cinnamon bun and a cup of filtered coffee or tea. Your awakening will taste completely different!

- **Rye bread** (rugbrød): the smell of freshly baked bread is certainly one of the most reassuring and good in the world. In Denmark, this intoxicating aroma takes the form of sandwich bread. It is dark, made with rye flour. The surface (sometimes even the crumb) is sprinkled with sunflower seeds. You can eat it simply with a layer of salted butter spread or make it the base of smørrebrød, the Scandinavian open bun. When it's a few days old, use it to make porridge.

- **Smørrebrød**: According to many, this simple slice of stuffed bread can give off positive vibes... it's a simple and rewarding way to have lunch. It is a dish that lends itself to a thousand variations and that can be easily shared with friends and family. Smoked or marinated salmon, boiled eggs and shrimp, pate, cheese, smoked mackerel, herring, avocado... all of which can make your lunch very Hygge. Are you ready to try it?

- **Gratin Dishes**: Fish (usually cod), cabbage or potatoes au gratin would make anyone feel at home, anywhere Here is the essence of Hygge! The ingredients, before being cooked and browned in the oven, are sautéed in a pan with butter and then covered with soft cream cheese or béchamel. Also very popular is the Bernese sauce, of French origin, prepared with egg yolk, butter and white wine.

- **Roast pork** (flæskesteg): This type of meat has always been one of the most popular ingredients in Denmark, along with fish, potatoes and cabbage. In particular, the roast pork is the typical dish that dominates the Danish tables for Christmas. The tasty and crunchy crust makes it inviting! As for the aromas, pepper and bay leaves are simply used and everything is served with cabbage and potatoes.

Chapter 14: Practical Hygge: How to customize your wardrobe

Hygge isn't just for your home or vacation, it's also for your daily life. According to some of the top Hygge experts (aka Meik Wiking, as mentioned in Chapter 1), almost everything you do and own can be "hygge'd". Therefore, fashion trends have also reached the explosion of popularity regarding this Danish lifestyle, and if you want to look - and feel - the part, designers and outlets have more than enough to offer. Likewise, making your wardrobe more Hygge in spirit doesn't have to cost a fortune, as the keyword is comfort - you probably have some hyggeligt items in your closet right now.

Keeping in line with all the information above on Hygge style, your Hygge wardrobe would be made up of neutral colors, some insist on lots of black and soft textures, with comfy scarves and socks galore. Layering clothing is also in the Hygge spirit, and that makes sense as the trend comes from cold winter weather.

Why Hygge your wardrobe? To help you feel an overall sense of well-being, to feel that your lifestyle is embracing you in a warm embrace, you need to feel warm and comfortable in all of your clothes. Learning to relax and stay in the present moment in everyday life requires clothes that are not fussy, that can be elegant without being uncomfortable, minimalist yet trendy. As with any wardrobe, there are excellent Hygge styles for the range of what you do, from going to a bar to biking or somersaulting in the park to hang out for dinner with the family. Anything in the Hygge style will be relaxed and comfortable, and the fact that the fashion world has caught on to this trend means that some of them can be quite beautiful in an understated way.

You want your clothes to match your mood. Just as your home décor creates an atmosphere conducive to the stress-free happiness of Hygge, so your wardrobe can set the stage for a Hygge feel that accompanies you everywhere.

The checklist

Knitwear is essential to the Hygge style. Not only is it convenient and cheap, but it's also easy to care for - no special care instructions, for the most part. Soft and fluid lines define the style.

Oversized garments are also very much in line with the Hygge trend, especially oversized sweaters. This is a style that never goes out of style, in any case, at least in the home. To go out, a neutral-colored cardigan is a perfect accessory to complete any outfit and to keep you warm all day.

Socks, Socks and More Socks: One of the main components of any Hygge wardrobe is a large supply of snug and comfortable socks, bulky to wear around the house, especially when you are curled up in your hyggekrog reading a book, and more stylish socks for girls.

Leisure sportswear has dominated the fashion industry for years; the Hygge touch on this is fleece wear. A little looser and softer, sweatpants free you from the stiffness of denim and can be dressed up or down, depending on the occasion. Try a comfortable blazer to dress them up or stick with an oversized sweater or cardigan for a more casual outfit.

Aside from the comfy socks, the most distinctive Hygge fashion element is the scarf. Like the oversized sweater, the scarf comes in an almost infinite variety of shapes and sizes, from large and voluminous to Harry Potter, or elegant and subtle. Whatever your preference, keep in mind that the scarf is not just a fashion accessory but a necessary piece of clothing in colder climates - scarves should be both practical and pretty to fit the Hygge spirit.

Also, don't ditch your sweater - or even your scarf - during the warmer months of spring or early fall. Instead, look for less bulky and/or shorter sweaters and elegant scarves of lightweight material to accentuate your look at any time of the year. The function of these is to give you a comfortable feeling of security, even if you don't need them for the practical purpose of heat.

The layering of the look is also very hyggeligt. Like the oversized sweater and voluminous scarf, layering can serve a very practical purpose and is also in keeping with the free spirit that underlies the Hygge philosophy. Plus, this is another nod to the actual climate that Hygge grows from - the weather in Denmark is notoriously changeable, so layering is an excellent way to be prepared for whatever weather comes your way. It might be gloomy as you go to the office, but sunny and warmer when you cycle to meet your friends at the local cafe, or vice versa. As a famous Danish proverb goes: "In Denmark there is no bad weather, only bad clothes."

Even the clothes to wear at home are hyggeligt. Keeping a dressing gown on hand for any season is a great way to invite self-care and moderate indulgence. Wearing a comfy robe out of the shower in the morning practically begs you to brew another cup of coffee or cocoa and sit in your cozy corner with a book or craft project. Invest in at least a couple, one for the warmer months and one for the coldest.

As previously mentioned, neutral colors are more in tune with the Hygge spirit than bold or bright colors and patterns. Light shades like beige and white are certainly Hygge, although black is another popular choice. Muted black, like charcoal, is part of the Hygge fashion. Wearing all black, especially in slightly different shades, is pretty chic without being harsh if it's done with Hygge in mind (i.e. loose, flowing, and layered).

A true import of Danish fashion is also a must-have for trendy Hygge acolytes: the style of the sweater worn by Sarah Lund, the protagonist of the immensely popular television series, The Killing. It can be described as a slightly oversized knitted sweater with a somewhat understated pattern. This is the perfect sweater for an afternoon outing during the colder months.

Remember: even if you go out for a more formal evening, it is possible to capture the spirit of Hygge - stay warm, first of all. Don't be afraid to layer a long, comfortable cardigan or wool jacket with an elegant dress for evening wear. If there's one thing Hygge doesn't support, it's the feeling of cold, as opposed to the well-being or warmth of a hug.

In terms of Hygge wardrobe, it is primarily a wardrobe that focuses on the same feeling of being in a cozy, warm and comfortable home. Therefore, the bulk of your Hygge wardrobe doesn't have to be stylish, new, or impressive. If you were to think in very trendy terms, you might think about coordinating your wardrobe with your interior design, both practical and in line with the Hygge spirit. Either way, you undoubtedly already have a handful of comfortable fleece sweaters, cardigans, and pants to wear every day at home; use them and invest in some cooler items to meet friends or go out for dinner. Now you have a personal Hygge style to take with you everywhere!

You can also think of Hygge beyond your wardrobe in your beauty regimen. The Hygge style is plain and simple, and that's exactly what your skincare and makeup regimen should be too. A neutral color palette, excellent moisturizers, and perhaps some essential oils and exfoliators are all you need to maintain a beautiful glow that comes from both the inside - practicing the happiness of Hygge - and the outside.

In the spirit of Hygge, celebrate life's little joys and stay present at all times - this shouldn't force you to think too much about your daily outfit, or feel obligated to dress up for someone else's ideals. Taking care of yourself means respecting yourself, just as you take the time to nurture your physical health. In this way, a Hygge wardrobe celebrates a woman's desire to look beautiful without submitting to the whims of others - other women, men or fashion magazines. That doesn't mean dressing up in Hygge style isn't attractive or sexy! Hygge clothing is simply designed by women for a woman's needs. It's cute and practical, comfortable and cozy - an excellent way to introduce yourself as a working woman, as a woman of means, as a mother, like a friend. It should express your style and common sense.

A Hygge mindset also means slowing down and reducing excess. Your wardrobe can - and should - express this; coordinating an excessive number of demanding accessories is not in the spirit of enjoying everyday life without clutter. Practical considerations should guide the choice of accessories rather than any kind of top-down fashionista thinking. This puts you in the driver's seat, pushing you to become an active consumer rather than a passive buyer. Again, practice can be nice, sometimes even cuter than a trick. So when considering your Hygge lifestyle, remember to let your natural beauty shine through, including through your clothing choice.

Hygge also means relaxation, avoiding the daily routine that often prompts people to succumb to external pressures and demands rather than internal joys and practical pleasures. It's hard to feel relaxed in restrictive clothing or so bright and bold that all eyes are always on you. Instead of working so diligently to impress others, we should work hard to help ourselves to happiness and serenity. One way to lower the pressures of everyday life is to allow yourself to wear loose, comfortable clothes that remind you how to maintain a sense of calm security.

Ultimately, Hygge, especially for working women, torn between so many conflicting demands, means being kinder to yourself. Giving yourself time, space and permission to relax and enjoy the simple pleasures in life are one of the greatest gifts you can give yourself. In this age of constant self-improvement, we are told that we must work harder and harder to become healthier and better. This mistake often reads as a simple thing, especially for women: thinner. While there is a contemporary rage for everything authentic (from food and craft beer to old-world crafts, repurposed furniture and handmade pickles), this new fashion tends to ignore women in terms of how it comes asked them to introduce themselves. Top models and movie stars dominate the pages of glossy magazines, movie screens and our televisions; for the most part, this idea of beauty is both unattainable and unhealthy. This is where the influence of Hygge makes itself felt slowly but surely. Over the past two decades, changes in social attitudes and the rapid growth of technology have allowed us to see many types of people in all shapes, sizes and profiles of beauty. Hygge is a trend that has embraced the idea that beauty is not simply an ideal and shouldn't be difficult or uncomfortable. It should be easy, cozy, comfortable and just you. This philosophy has been a driving force behind Danish culture for many years, and led to one of the most feminine cultures in the world, not to mention the birth of the happiest people on earth! Hygge is not just a fad, but a true lifestyle that could teach us a little about self-love and kindness.

Chapter 15: Practical Hygge: Hungry for Hygge

As with any long-standing tradition in any culture in the world, food plays a significant role. It would be difficult to think of Thanksgiving without turkey, for example, or imagine St. Patrick's Day without bread and beer. In addition to these centuries-old examples, cultures with deeply rooted religious traditions also have accompanying foods, such as matzo during Passover or dates for breaking the daily fast during Ramadan. Denmark is predominantly Christian in its religious traditions, and in the next chapter we will discuss how Hygge and the holidays - Christmas and Easter, for example - work together in the next chapter.

What makes a food hyggeligt? Warm, Cozy Foods fit the category on a T-shirt: Just as the word Hygge can be etymologically traced to "hug," the foods you eat while practicing Hygge should represent a hug from the inside out. Because Hygge is also about communion between family and friends, hyggeligt food is meant to be shared with loved ones at the dinner table, with lots of conversation and interactions. This can be in a bar, eating some fika (snacks to be consumed with hot drinks), or it can be at your home, enjoying a homemade dinner. Hygge doesn't deal directly with health - a sugar sandwich is a lot of Hygge while celery sticks are - but it encourages restraint. The Hygge emphasis on Outdoor activity balances the significant consumption of cocoa and sweets, or at least that's the idea! Eating hyggeligt is not about guilt or self-control; it concerns health in the sense of self-care, comfort and communion with others. Breaking bread with others has always been a sacrosanct act, and Hygge emphasizes the joys and pleasures of sharing food around a crowded table.

Focaccia and bread for breakfast

By hearsay, breakfast is the most important meal of the day and this couldn't be more true when you start your hyggeligt day. A large steaming cup of coffee or cocoa (or tea, if you prefer) is a must to get you going on a cold morning, accompanied by a hearty breakfast to fuel you on your bike ride, for your daily work or just to encourage you to light a fire before settling in your cozy corner with a good book. The following recipes are just a quick representation of all that Danish food has to offer to break the fast every morning. Remember: Hygge food doesn't have to be exclusively Danish!

Note: All recipes in this chapter are represented as a set of instructions, more method than the recipe in traditional cookbook jargon. Read each step carefully before gathering the ingredients and starting to cook.

Rugbrød: Danish rye bread

Makes two loaves

This traditional recipe seems a little intimidating at first, but once you get past the ingredients list and get used to making a sourdough starter, this is a delicious and hearty bread for any time of day.

- Mix together with a scant cup of broken rye grains, broken wheat, flax seeds, and sunflower seeds. To this, add 1 1/2 cups of sourdough (there are many easy ways to do this, using only yeast, flour and water - the internet has a variety of recipes), 3 cups of water and 1-2 tablespoons of malt syrup (the molasses will be fine in a pinch). Combine all of these ingredients the night before making the loaves, leaving everything to soak for about 8 hours.
- The next morning, add 1 1/2 cups of rye flour and all-purpose flour, along with 1 tablespoon of salt. Let the dough rise for about 1 hour and a half.

- Bake the loaves in two standard bread pans in a preheated oven at 350 degrees for about an hour. Take your loves out of the pans, letting them cool down a bit before slicing them and spreading them with butter or yogurt or salted/sweetened jam.

Porridge: staple food

Although many things could be called Denmark's national dish, porridge would be in the running. There are as many recipes for porridge as there are Danes themselves! Here is a simple take on this classic food, far beyond American childhood microwave oatmeal.

- For one serving, mix about 4 ½ ounces of oatmeal (or other substantial grains, like spelled, spelled or quinoa - cooking times will vary, of course) with a cup of water in a small saucepan. Add a diced and core apple and ½ cup of berries (blueberries, blackberries, raspberries), along with 1/3 cup of chopped walnuts, almonds, pecans, or walnuts work well. Add a pinch or two of salt and leave to simmer until the grains have thickened and are tender. Once the heat is out, serve with a few splashes of milk or cream - or a dollop of yogurt - and add a pinch of salt for a savory taste. You could add some honey for sweetness.

As you can see, this recipe is a basic method of building to your taste and what goes on in your pantry or refrigerator. In keeping with the tradition of frugality, Danes also like to make porridge with stale rugbrød, with raisins, dried citrus peel, honey and hot spices.

Ebleskivers: Danish pancakes

Makes about three dozen

These fluffy pancake-like creations could be served for afternoon tea - or fika, as it's commonly called in Denmark - as well as for breakfast. Although a special ebleskiver pan is available to encourage these cakes to keep a cookie-like shape and help them rise, you can easily cook them in a pan or griddle like traditional American-style pancakes.

- Whisk together 2 cups of flour, one teaspoon each of baking soda and baking soda, a generous pinch of salt and a ¼ teaspoon of cinnamon in a large bowl. Set it aside while you prepare the wet ingredients.
- In another bowl, beat 3 egg whites until stiff peaks form - this will help the ebleskivers rise and contribute to their lightness.

- In another bowl, beat the 3 egg yolks with a couple of tablespoons of sugar until incorporated, then slowly beat in 2 cups of buttermilk and 2 teaspoons of vanilla. Stir in the dry ingredients and then gently add the beaten egg whites.
- For each small pancake, use a round spoonful of batter. To each, add a teaspoon of finely diced fruit - peeled apples are the most traditional, but you can also use peaches, pears, or even small berries. Cook on a well-oiled griddle, skillet, or skillet until the edges start to boil and the bottom begins to turn slightly golden. Turn and cook for another minute, then serve dusted with powdered sugar or covered with a spoonful of whipped cream.

Lunch and lighter fare

Lunch is usually a lighter affair in Denmark, being in between the two beloved traditions of a hearty, hot breakfast and afternoon coffee delights for fika (coffee and a sweet snack). The recipes below provide just a quick example of what might be on the menu, but there are countless variations on these themes. The smørrebrød category itself is simply a blank canvas for any number of ingredients, and the soup's popularity offers a dizzying array of options, from squash/squash to cauliflower to split pea - the list goes on! Plus, lunch could also be a hearty vegetable casserole or a savory variant of porridge. A lot of popular American dishes could be considered a very Hygge lunch: macaroni and cheese, for example, or a large bowl of pasta with ragù or pesto, or the ever-popular Chicken Pot Pie; these are all warm, simple yet delicious dishes that are very much in line with the spirit of Hygge.

Smørrebrød: Infinite Variety

Smørrebrød essentially refers to an open-faced sandwich, usually eaten with a knife and fork, topped with an almost infinite variety of meats, cheeses, vegetables, and so on. These lunchtime delicacies are inevitably linked to the Scandinavian countries, where they are a symbol of the simplicity and conviviality of the various peoples who reside there. Start with a fairly thick slice of good bread - your choice, although rye is traditional for most smørrebrøds - then spread it with some rich butter, topping it all off with favorite ingredients.

Some combinations you might try:

- o Cold smoked salmon with thinly sliced cucumber and plenty of chopped fresh dill;
- o Sliced boiled egg with avocado spears and thinly sliced radishes;

- Herring paté or pickled liver with thinly sliced red onion and chopped parsley;
- Good Havarti cheese with sliced tomato and chopped chives;
- Cold cuts, such as salami or ham, with onions, tomatoes and/or herbs.

In short, almost anything you have in your refrigerator and/or garden would work in these open sandwiches. Just don't forget the smudge of butter and the friendliness of the toppings. After all, this is a knife and fork business.

Tomato soup, Nordic style

8-10 servings

Most - and I mean 99.99 percent - of American children enjoyed the staple lunchtime food of hot tomato soup with grilled cheese. It's a classic, both made from a can of Campbell soup with Wonder Bread and a wedge of cheese wrapped in plastic, or from some roasted garden tomatoes with local sourdough bread wrapped around artisanal cheddar. It's also very, very Hygge: warm, comforting, familiar, simple, and deliciously delicious. The following recipe is a more Danish version of that classic combination.

- Chop 1 onion, 2 or 3 cloves of garlic, half a pound of celeriac (celery root) and a couple of carrots, then brown together in a large pot in 3 tablespoons of olive oil until everything is softened a little.
- Add 3 cups of chopped tomatoes (canned will do fine), 2 tablespoons of tomato paste, 1 cup of wine (usually a dry white, but you can experiment), and about 8 cups of broth. Homemade broth is always the best, of course, but whatever you have the time for; remember this is hygge cooking and we shouldn't be stressed about it! For a more traditional or vegan version, consider using vegetable or mushroom broth.
- Cook everything together until all the vegetables are cooked and tender and the soup thickens slightly for about ten to fifteen minutes. Serve with mixed cooked rye berries or a couple of thick slices of rugbrød, spread with butter or topped with Edam cheese and grilled.

Hot Smoked Salmon: Scandinavian staple

For 4 people

Salmon, along with herring, is also a clear sign of Scandinavian food, which is omnipresent throughout the region. Cold smoked salmon is best left to the experts unless you have the specialized equipment, but hot-smoked salmon can easily be prepared in a home kitchen. Pair it with a nice green salad and you have a satisfying meal.

- Make a cure for half a kilo of salmon. You can use any type of fish, such as a firm, oily fish like rainbow trout, but sockeye with skin is perhaps the most popular. Combine 2 cups of brown sugar with 1 cup of kosher salt, 1 tablespoon of freshly ground black pepper, and one teaspoon each of ground coriander seeds and juniper berries.

Optional: Add the grated zest of a couple of oranges for bright sweetness. Let it dry in the refrigerator for a couple of hours.

- Prepare your smoker. There are inexpensive, commercially available stove smokers that are very easy to use and these are worth the small investment if you plan on doing it more than a couple of times a year. They are also great for smoking shellfish, tomatoes and other vegetables, as well as small pieces of meat. If you don't have one, make a makeshift smoker by using a heavy skillet with a lid, aluminum foil, and some wood chips or dried tea leaves. To do this, put a layer of aluminum foil in the pan, then sprinkle the wood chips on this layer. You can use whole tea and spices with chips or in place of chips; in both cases it gives flavor to your mea/fish. On top of the chips or spices, spread another layer of aluminum foil. Place the salmon in a steamer basket or tray, lower it into the smoker and cover with the lid. Turn the heat up to high and watch, with the lid ajar, until you see puffs of smoke come out of the pan. Cover tightly, lower the heat to medium heat so as not to burn the chips too quickly. If desired, baste a few times with maple syrup for a lacquered look and a sweeter taste. Smoke the salmon for about 40 minutes until it flakes easily with a fork. If desired, baste a few times with maple syrup for a lacquered look and sweeter taste.

Chapter 16: Practical Hygge: Holidays and Hygge Seasons

Although Hygge is associated with the holiday season and winter, it is certainly possible to practice it at any time of the year. Indeed, as this philosophy becomes more popular around the world, many people apply Hygge principles to holidays, festivals, and seasonal activities throughout the year. The Danes would suggest that this is right, as Hygge is a mindset, not a fleeting state of mind. Every day is a good day for Hygge, and in this chapter you will find ideas on how to keep yourself engaged with the Hygge spirit. Winter: Hyggeligt season!

For too many of us, winter is a time of fear, with cold and windy weather, complicated travel, holiday pressures, bored or sick children stuck indoors. For Danes who embrace the Hygge philosophy, winter can be the most magical, comforting and welcoming time of the year. The essence of Hygge truly embodies what we love most about winter: wrapping up in a blanket in front of a fire, wearing comfy socks, cooking comforting foods, and taking some time off your busy schedule for some relaxation, take care of yourself and celebrate the family. No time of year is more suitable for indulging in Hygge. Below are some ideas on how to make your winter Hygge.

- Since you can't spend too much time outside, bring nature inside - potted poinsettias are a holiday tradition that brightens and soothes your home sanctuary.
- If you spend time outdoors, invest in (or create) a fire pit; there's nothing more Hygge than getting together around a roaring fire and roasting marshmallows with friends and family.
- Also, don't forget about winter sports - if you're lucky enough to live where snowfall is adequate, take the family on sledding, skiing, or ice skating. These are excellent ways to bond as a family and make the most of the colder weather while engaging in a healthy outdoor activity.
- Consider an overnight snow trek, with or without snowshoes, depending on the area, as there is nothing quite as magical as the glow of the moon on freshly fallen snow.

- If the cold finally gets you down, take refuge in a bar. You would have done it anyway, right? It is a daily activity! Level up and instead of your usual haunt, visit a museum and grab your afternoon fika in their cafe; most of the larger museums now have a small place to eat on the grounds.
- Create your visual memories by taking out your camera to snap some nature and family photos. Put together an album to share with everyone.

- Don't forget our fellow men: it's cold for everyone! Set aside some food or a bird feeder and spend some time watching and learning - an excellent way to get kids involved in nature activities.
- Think of your home bathroom like a spa retreat: invest in a bubble bath or bath salts, play some soothing music, and have a soft, warm dressing gown wait at the end of a relaxing bath.
- Remember that winter foods aren't limited to holidays. There's no better time of year to indulge in a cup of cocoa on a winter's day, breaking the old fondue pot and inviting your friends to a party. Make sure you also have mulled wine or cider on hand.
- Face the pile of books on your nightstand - prepare a hyggekrog (cozy corner) and allow yourself a few happy hours of leisurely reading. And, by the way, real books with some weight are much more hyggeligt than reading on an electronic device. I'm just saying...
- Spend a day in pajamas where the whole family stays and relaxes, ideally indulging in both group activities. Board games, anyone? Movie marathon with popcorn and sweets? If it's not a group meeting, everyone can curl up with the books.
- Start a jar of treasure. While this can be done at any time of the year, it is especially powerful during the

winter to see how nature changes from autumn to spring. Collect small items from your daily walk or bike ride (you know, your Hygge business) and store them in a jar. At the end of the season, organize and display your new treasures.

- Learn something new or teach something new - or both. Cook with your kids, sign up for a class on something you've always wanted to learn, or teach yourself a different language.
- Observe the stars, figuratively and literally. Plan for the next season, design your dream garden for spring, think about your summer vacation, etc. Make sure you don't forget to look up into the clear night sky and treasure the present (gratitude!) and dream about the future.

Christmas is the most beautiful Hyggeligt time of the year

In the mainly Christian countries of the north, the holiday most associated with winter is Christmas. With this holiday comes a host of traditions that are very hyggeligt - the very idea of upholding and creating tradition is part of the Hygge spirit itself. Even if you celebrate another seasonal holiday (for example,

Hanukkah or Kwanzaa), you can adapt some of these traditions for your enjoyment.

- Lights, lights and more lights! Fairy lights or twinkling lights can adorn any room in the house, along with candles and Christmas tree lights. Put them in clear jars or tuck them on shelves or wrap them around railings.
- Write letters to Santa Claus with your children. Encourage them to think of these letters not only as personal wish lists of material items, but also lists of what to be thankful for and what to expect in the New Year.
- Decorate the house both indoors and out with seasonal items: reindeer and trees, elves and snowmen, lights and ornaments, wreaths and garlands. Make it a family business and get everyone involved in creating a special setting for a special time of year.
- Throw a closing party with family or friends (or both). Ask everyone to develop their special skills, whether it's coordinating paper and ribbon, making bows, or using special characters for gift cards.
- Give Homemade Gifts: Jams and jellies, pickles and preserves, liqueurs and flavored libations are all welcome gifts for hostesses this time of year. If you have other skills, use these too: sketch a drawing, paint a picture, or write and frame a poem. The pottery and woodworking

crafts are also fabulous. These types of handmade gifts are truly priceless.

- Go see a Christmas show with the family, whether it's the local production of The Nutcracker or the latest Christmas-themed movie. While you're at it, listen to some Christmas carols or take the family to sing around the neighborhood.

- A new tradition begins to return to every year: decorating personalized mugs for each member of the family; knit hats or scarves for friends, gift dated ornaments to the special people in your life, organize a movie weekend for marathon holidays or organize Christmas Eve brunch for neighbors and friends.

Spring: renew and invigorate

After the comforts (and challenges) of the winter passage, many people are looking forward to spring. It is of course the time of year when our thoughts turn to renewal and rebirth; the birds begin to sing again, the earth awakens and we return to the open-air with renewed vigor. All these typical spring sensations are completely compatible with the Hygge philosophy: working outdoors, playing outdoors, observing and respecting nature, feeling gratitude for the small miracles in our daily life, approaching a fulfilling project that allows us to spend time with family and friends.

- First of all, don't abandon your candles! There is nothing that says cute in spring-like little tea candles on a picnic table or in your dining room. Choose fresh but muted colors, such as peach and light green for a recognition of the natural scene that is awakening outdoors. This lighting, in addition to opening the windows and letting in fresh air and natural light, will keep you in the Hygge spirit every day.
- Flowers should also be part of your Hygge spring. And most importantly, these flowers should be natural, found just outside your door - even the humblest looking grass-like flower is beautiful in the right arrangement and under straight gaze! Wildflowers in glass jars safely evoke spring Hygge.
- Play in the dirt! One of the most wonderful things about spring is the opportunity to get out and get your hands dirty - plant a garden, build a treehouse, or add more trees or hedges. Build something for the future in glorious spring weather.
- Speaking of outdoor activities, be sure to have a picnic or two or ten, while the weather is perfect for these things. Fly a kite, play in the park, notice the ducklings hatching

and the butterflies emerging. Introduce your children to the wonders of spring rebirth.

• Speaking of outdoor activities in bad weather, be sure to play in the rain! A gentle spring rain is one of the most beautiful sensations in the world, especially for a small child in all its wonder. And if you live in an area with a fierce spring climate - and this is most of us - enjoy it as if you enjoy the winter. Wonder; to the power of nature while you're in your safe haven with your loved ones. These are the days built for hyggekrogs and reading binges.

• Look at your home decor and think about spring. Keep it minimalist and tidy, as he'd like us to do Hygge, but bring some lighter, a little brighter pieces to suit the changing seasons outside. Put some crisp sheets on your bed and swap your ultra fuzzy robe for a shiny silk one to welcome in the warmer season.

• As for the cuisine, spring Hygge is about the market. Go to the local farmers' market and indulge in all the rare and fleeting spring delicacies like fresh strawberries and asparagus, broad beans and sweet peas, lettuce and delicate herbs, spring chickens and their glorious eggs. There's a reason Easter celebrations typically feature deviled eggs and young lamb - it's just the right season for that. Check out other Easter ideas below.

Easter Redux

Perhaps the ultimate celebration of renewal and rebirth is the sacred feast of Easter. No matter how you celebrate it, Easter is a beautiful spring opportunity to gather with family and friends around a table laden with food, sharing gratitude for all that we are lucky enough to have.

Even if you're not celebrating Easter, there are ample opportunities to kickstart a centuries-old spring festival, with some or all of the ideas below:

- Secret Snowdrop Letters: This is a Danish tradition at Easter, to send a craft paper letter to a loved one, with a sweet and thoughtful message, left unsigned. Tradition says that if the recipient guesses that you sent the letter, you have to give him an Easter egg; if they can't guess who sent it, they have to give you an Easter egg. It's kind of like a secret Santa for spring. The trick is to cut out a beautiful paper design, as you could have done (depending on your age) in school with hearts for Valentine's Day or a chain of paper daisies.
- In terms of holiday decorations, many Danes will even set up some kind of Easter tree with spring branches and other natural material. It is adorned with symbols of

fertility (such as eggs) and rebirth (such as feathers and flowers).

• Speaking of eggs, certainly every Easter celebration is private without the traditional colored eggs, of course, but to be extra-Hygge, choose natural dyes that come from common kitchen items rather than chemicals (for example: beet juice or chlorophyll extract). And of course, you will be doing this with children, family and/or friends around your dining table.

• Go on an Easter egg hunt, but try to make sure it's out. Sometimes the spring weather forbids it, as people in my region know! Every two years, Easter seems to be cold and forbidden outside. However, if possible, gather to hunt outside. If not out, don't worry! The idea of a playful task for kids is Hygge in and of itself.

• Don't forget to enjoy some special Easter treats as well, the kinds of chocolate treats that only come once a year - all the better if they're homemade, of course, but some purchased treats can also become an annual tradition.

• Speaking of food, an Easter party is always a must! It can be one of the sweet teeth of the year and the food itself is hyggeligt in its very nature: fresh spring veggies, a large comforting ham or spring leg of lamb, lush deviled eggs (to use all handsomely dyed ones), braided Easter bread and delicious desserts. Make sure you have a beautiful centerpiece made from natural spring branches and other found materials. And candles! And many friends and relatives.

• Homemade Easter decorations are a treat and a way to practice Hygge with your kids and others. It is also very useful to give gifts for your annual Easter baskets, whether they are edible or handcrafted - this shows how much you care about your children or other people you give gifts to.

And don't forget Mother's Day, another day to give your mom a Hygge experience!

Summer: the outdoors is ours

Since every time of the year is a time for Hygge and since summer is the time for holidays, relaxation and outdoor activities, it could be said that this is the hyggeligt time of the year, beyond out winter. Most people take some time off in the summer, and it is the time of year for many friendly outdoor gatherings with fun and sunshine. They may not be comfortable socks and blankets, but that doesn't mean you can't Hygge your outdoor spaces and indoor activities.

• Lighten up your linens so you feel free to enjoy the luxury in bed all morning. Indeed, why not indulge - or a loved one - a breakfast in bed? Make your bedroom a bright and welcoming space for exactly the kind of rechargeable relaxation we could all use at any time of the year.

- Use your porch or create one, as best you can. Create a hyggekrog that receives the best sunlight and install a comfortable sofa or lazy armchair with lots of cushions, cushions and natural lighting. This is the place to read the summer readings.
- Speaking of summer reading, this is the time of year to indulge in a light and airy reading, whatever it means to you: romantic comedies, mysteries, memoirs. Leave the studio at another time of the year.
- Experience life in the garden as much as possible: Create a space in your backyard where everyone feels comfortable gravitating. Make sure there are comfortable seats, enough for everyone, and natural furniture for everyone.
- Outdoor dining, of course, in your cozy backyard space, weather and insects permitting. Put some lemongrass to help with the bugs to make it a safe space for everyone.
- Set up a hammock and have deck chairs, as this is the time of year to relax, preferably with a nice cup of tea or a glass of wine. Part of the Hygge spirit is to slow down and enjoy each day; this is the perfect environment to do it.

- Go camping and toast hot dogs and marshmallows around the fire with your friends and family. If you're lucky, you'll have a nearby beach where you can enjoy a sunny day full of fun and play, followed by a warm night of good conversation and glorious summer food.
- Collect shells along the beach and make a wreath or necklace or centerpiece for your dining table at home.
- If you can, take a vacation. Better yet - and even more hyggeligt - take a stay, turning your home into a weekend or week-long vacation.
- Finally, remember a key component of the Hygge philosophy: it's not about financial investment; it's about the experience itself.

Festival of the days, from memorial to work

Summer is also filled with potential celebratory holidays, most of which are centuries-old holidays enjoyed by most Americans. Memorial Day, at the end of May, kicks off the summer season semi-officially, followed by Father's Day in June and Independence Day in July. The summer season semi-officially ends with the Labor Day holiday in early September. These celebrations are centered all around America; however, any excuse to host a party or to practice Hygge with family and friends is almost always a good one. Consider some of the following ideas on how to hygge-fy your summer vacation:

- Memorial Day is primarily a day of remembrance for fallen soldiers and veterans who sacrificed a lot for our country; it is in the spirit of gratitude that we should face the day. It is also the perfect time of year, from a weather perspective, to communicate with family and friends during an outdoor gathering, usually a backyard barbecue. Spend the day placing flags and flowers on graves, attend a veteran service and/or visit your veteran family and friends, this spirit of gratitude is very Hygge. Then, spend the evening bonding with family and friends at a large garden party, using some of the tips mentioned above.

- Father's Day is also a day to express gratitude to the fathers who raised and guided you. Remember that we may all have more of our biological fathers to honor on a day like this; perhaps a dear grandfather or uncle, an adoptive father or stepfather or a prominent mentor. Make a card or a homemade gift to send your father figures and be sure to let them know how much they mean to you. This can often take the form of another backyard barbecue or another type of family reunion where the food is simple and the company is great.

- Independence Day is a celebration of America's history and independence and another occasion to express gratitude. It is also an opportunity to spend some time with family and friends and some good food. Fireworks are perhaps a bit flashy for the normally subdued spirit of the Hygge, but in this case the exuberance is well placed. To make the fourth more hyggeligt, give yourself a day at the beach, some time to reflect and get together with the others at the party. Plus, grill some Hygge food, like burgers and ribs!
- Labor Day honors the hard work we all have done throughout the year. It could easily be argued that if Hygge were a more ingrained part of American culture, we wouldn't need a Labor Day vacation at all every day would be a way to enjoy work-life balance. Either way, keep in mind that Labor Day is the end of one season and the start of another, usually busier, time of year. Honor it by reminding yourself that the practice of Hygge can be followed throughout the year, even with the start of school and the lazy days of summer over. The Labor Day party is the perfect time to engage in Hygge practice during the fall and glorious winter.

Autumn: Cozy Up

While to some autumn may seem like the end of the long vacation that is summer, to others - and this means that we, with our hyggeligt vision - it can represent the long and slow slide into the more welcoming seasons. The autumn weather is cool and we start pulling out our oversized sweaters and comfy socks. Fall colors are naturally beautiful so we incorporate them into our home decor. Autumn evenings are quiet and calm, perfect for postprandial walks. Autumn is the season when the shops start closing earlier, taking us back to the safe havens of our homes. It is one of the most beautiful times of the year. Below are some unique activities and ideas to bring more Hygge into your season.

- Do some fall planting - there are lots of crops and plants that like to spend the winter snuggling underground, so here's your last chance of the year to get your hands dirty in the garden! Tulips are one such flower that likes to overwinter and are a beautiful symbol of spring. If you like vegetable gardens, then planting tubers and other root vegetables is the thing to do.

Wintering garlic is one of the funniest and easiest types of planting to do!

- Think of the cornucopia symbol: Autumn is the time to show gratitude for the abundance, the prolific harvest.

Store and Preserve: Don't waste the end-of-season bounty you have around you. Share your size with family, friends and neighbors.

- Go pick apples; take the family outdoors to enjoy the perfect time of year for this most symbolic of fruit. Later that night, have a caramel apple contest, bake some caramel apples for a divine fall treat or both.
- Take a road trip to enjoy the changing seasons and the explosion of autumn colors. Be sure to pack a picnic or two along the way, and sit under a tree while watching the leaves gently slide to the ground.
- Say Hello to Pumpkin: One of the enduring symbols of autumn, pumpkin and various other pumpkins come into the picture this time of year. In addition to the whole pumpkin thing, you can also make pumpkin bread, pie, soup, and a whole host of other hyggeligt recipes designed to get the best out of this sacred vegetable.
- Start knitting or learn how - this is the time of year to start your projects for winter and gift season.
- Autumn is also a wonderful time of the year to take pictures in nature; the light is the right one most days and the beautiful colors create wonderful photos.
- Organize a treasure hunt! Smarter and more adult than Halloween, a scavenger hunt is the perfect fall activity for a group of game friends. Go out, enjoy, then be sure to

offer some large bowls of soup and pieces of crusty bread to enjoy - along with a good conversation - at the end of the evening.

Thanksgiving isn't just for Americans

The autumn season is not as full of holidays, secular or not, as the other seasons. For Americans, Thanksgiving is of great importance: it is both a nationally celebrated holiday that crosses all religious and cultural lines and the official start of the great holiday season which is winter. Even if you're not American - or if you find the Thanksgiving myth a little too blanched for your liking - you can still appreciate the message below of thanks for everything we've enjoyed throughout the year. For most Americans, Thanksgiving means certain foods and family reunions, and this is certainly in the spirit of Hygge too: tradition and gratitude are key components of living the Hygge lifestyle. Then, roast the turkey and stuffing if you like, or just invite friends and family over for a potluck dinner. Either way, you are practicing the greatest simple joys of Hygge.

Chapter 17: Practical Hygge: Parenting, Relationships, and Solidarity

One of the most crucial components in the practice of Hygge is to encourage and facilitate positive relationships, fostering togetherness. Practicing Hygge can have a profound impact on all of your relationships, from parenting with empathy to cultivating a marital bond to becoming a better friend. The hyggeligt traditions of socializing in cafes and eating family dinners around a set table create bonds of affection that last a lifetime. Hygge activities also emphasize the importance of spending time with our loved ones with joy and attention. Embracing the simplicity and pleasure of every day is deeply comforting for all of us, especially children, and recognizing that our highest forms of happiness arise from our relationships with others remains at the heart of the Hygge lifestyle.

Parents: Peaceful parenting

The impact we have as parents cannot be overstated, of course, and how we decide to be parents not only affects our children's physical and psychological health, but also serves as a model for how our children behave and interact with the others out in the world. Eventually, in most cases, this carries over to how your children are parents of their children. The Hygge way of parenting emphasizes solidarity, authenticity and empathy. It may seem, at first glance, that the Hygge lifestyle is for the carefree and childless: afternoons spent lounging in cafes or in front of the fire or binge-reading in a cozy, quiet corner. However, the underlying values inherent in the concept of Hygge can be applied quite appropriately to parenting styles. "Who among us wouldn't embrace the idea of "peaceful parenting?"

- One of the most important parenting techniques you can employ is that of being present with your children. Tune in to their needs and wants, rather than trying to project onto them what you think they might need or want. Get down on their level - literally - and see the world through their eyes.

- Be sincere and authentic when responding to their interests. Any child of reasonable acuity knows when an adult condescends to them, so respond with genuine questions and support.

- Empathy is also a central tenant in Hygge-style parenting (and living, in general); fostering an empathy of others by demonstrating this to your children creates a bond like no other.

- Encourage creative activity: get involved in art projects with your children or play dress-up or make-believe. Nurture their imagination and create a safe space for them to express themselves. Believe it or not, you will gain as much from this interaction as they do.
- Encourage play that is stimulating to the senses. While technological devices and computers have a place in our lives, to be sure, there is something to be said for more traditional kinds of tactile play. Consider investing in a sandbox, make models, or play with dough.
- Music is also an excellent way to get kids - and yourself - up and moving, while stimulating our bodies and minds. Physical activity is as important to brain development and overall health as is intellectual pursuits.
- Always eat together and encourage your children to participate. This ritual cannot be stressed enough! This habit of spending time preparing food, giving thanks, and eating around a table together is a habit for life. Study after study shows the amazing benefits that this one simple ritual can have on children. It makes for more humane, empathetic, and grateful interactions for the rest of their lives.
- Playing games together is another key component in fostering a child into adulthood. Games often provide

practice for real-life - at least in traditional games. With this in mind, try weaning kids away from the phone and the computer, engaging them in other forms of play that help them to model relationships and activities that will assist them in adulthood.

- Don't forget to play outside, as well. Nurture a love of the outdoors and empathy for nature, in general. Remember the Danish saying: there is no bad weather, only bad clothing choices. Outdoor play is a year-round affair, and in any season, there is always the reward of returning to the safe haven of the home, either for a mug of cocoa and a bowl of soup or for some lemonade and a smørrebrød spread.
- Read together - another surefire way to create a lifelong, positive habit! Encourage children to spend quiet time reading along, as well.

Allow children the space to figure out their self-care.

- Spend some time with physical affection, too. Snuggling and comforting your children is one the most significant things you can do to make them feel safe and happy throughout their lives. When you give them your full attention and engagement, you give them peace and happiness.
- Finally, remember to believe in yourself: trusting your Hygge instincts as a parent will give you the confidence,

kindness, and patience to nurture your children with love and generosity.

Partners: Nurturing Relationships

We would also do well to consider the foundations of a Hygge lifestyle when approaching our partners, whether they are spouses, significant others, or co-parents. We often forget that relationships take effort, just as raising children to do. Without the same kind of nurturing spirit with which we approach our children, relationships can stagnate or grow untenable. The concept of Hygge is easily applicable to our romantic relationships, and many of the basic tenants of Hygge in and of themselves will foster a healthy connection. For example, creating a comforting and cozy home is a first step toward coming home from work into a welcoming environment, the kind of place where a good mood is easy to come by. Other tips and techniques for maintaining happy love relationships are as follows.

- Create good energy throughout your house, especially the places in which you interact at an intimate level, such as the bedroom. The living area is for everyone who enters your house, but the bedroom should be a place that is hygge-fied just for the two of you.

- Fill your home with items that have meaning, rather than material objects that simply advertise wealth or success. You can't buy Hygge; instead, you build it via memory-making and attention to the mundane details of the everyday. Family photographs, mementos from vacations, natural found objects decorate your space in such a way that cements togetherness.
- But don't forget yourself. One of the foundational elements in creating a Hygge relationship is to embody Hygge ideals yourself. Self-care is necessary to care for anyone else. Also, think of this in terms of your house: it should remind you not only of your present togetherness, but also of yourself. Losing yourself in a relationship is not a formula for happiness, but rather a recipe for long-term resentments.
- Communication, as we all well know, is key to any constructive relationship. Learn to communicate openly, honestly, authentically, and calmly for best results.
- Cooperation is also key to any successful relationship, especially if it involves multiple people and objectives: partners raising children together invariably must cooperate on many fronts, but you also must learn to cooperate within the confines of your one interpersonal relationship. This is reliant on open and honest

communication and a desire to put togetherness ahead of other goals.

- Leave work at work. This is harder to do than it sounds for many, if not most of us. However, if you are to create a relationship with true togetherness that embodies the spirit of Hygge, then you must pay attention to how your working life invades your home life. Try to achieve as much balance as you can, and if you simply must address work issues at the home, try to follow some simple rules. Do not interrupt family time around the dinner table with work. Designate a specific area of the house - not the bedroom - in which work might be briefly conducted. Finish any work at least an hour before you plan to get to sleep, so you won't sacrifice evening bonding.
- Speaking of dinner, that time is sacred, something to be protected and honored. Make it a habit to keep it sacred.
- Use music to set the mood: curate your playlists for different occasions, different seasons to keep you in the spirit of relaxed happiness.
- Slowing down, in general, is the rule of thumb when practicing Hygge. Make special time for your significant other daily, no matter how seemingly simple or limited this might be. Hold hands while watching a movie, take

a walk after dinner, commit to an hour before bedtime alone without interruption.

- Minimize the excess stuff in your lives, whether it is material or emotional. The baggage of all kinds interferes with peace and happiness.

Friends: Establishing Bonds

Another crucial factor in practicing Hygge is to form and maintain friendship bonds. Besides your family, friends are the most important connections you have in the world, and ideally, friends fulfill needs that family cannot. Talking to a friend about the stresses you have in raising children is quite different than having that same discussion with a co-parent. Having some time away from family is just as healthy and important as spending quality time with them. Friendships are our way of keeping a sense of our own self separate from the needs and desires of family members. And, just as with children and with intimate relationships, friendships must be nurtured and cultivated with warmth and attention to maintain. One of the most striking facts to emerge out of recent sociological research is that social connection is the best predictor of overall happiness. Thus, we need to establish and maintain the bonds we have with our strongest social connections via friendships and other extended relationships.

- Make time to spend with friends regularly. It's wonderful if you can establish a standing date and time to meet with friends each week or create a ritual in which friendly interactions take place with spontaneity and ease. The café culture in Denmark creates a kind of built-in experience in which to foster friendships; if you don't have that kind of thing where you live, think of other places/ways in which friendly meetings can happen (a diner, a bookshop, a casual bar).
- Invest in friendships by welcoming them into your home: host a monthly Sunday brunch, or Saturday game night, or Friday night card game, or wine Wednesdays, or thirsty Thursdays - whatever works best for your crowd. The point is to make the event a recurring one rather than an occasional one; planning and fuss are kept to a minimum, and your house becomes the welcoming, comforting place to be.
- Encourage drop-ins. This is not a typically American attitude in our contemporary society, where we often don't even know our neighbors, but this is an ingrained part of Danish life. If your home is hygge-fied, then you may find that it happens anyway.

- Don't worry about throwing big, elaborate parties to bond with friends. Oftentimes, the most intimate bonding happens with just a handful of people, ideally being three to five. Also, this isn't the point of hyggeligt togetherness anyway; the point is to be relaxed, comfortable, and casual wherein great company can be readily enjoyed.
- But do always have good food and drinks on hand. This doesn't have to be fancy, to reiterate, but in the spirit of hospitality, honor your friends with generosity and kindness.
- Savor the moment: envision time with friends as you would time with family, a time to unplug from devices and to interact with conviviality and conversation.
- Remember that friendship is a choice, unlike family, and with those choices come a dedication to caring for others outside of your immediate family. This kind of thinking has a definite ripple effect, radiating out from family to friends to neighbors to strangers. Fostering mutual respect and empathetic connection among peoples is at the heart of practicing Hygge.

Family: Intergenerational Togetherness

Everything that can be said above about friendship and most of what can be said about our family relationships also applies to extended family. One of the tragedies of modern American life is that we spend more time with technology than ever and less time with our extended families and elders. So much wisdom is to be gained from maintaining relationships and connection with our grandparents, aunts, uncles, mentors, and others. While this is certainly not relegated just to Hygge practice, the relationships that we can foster with extended family members enrich, enlighten, and enliven our lives in innumerable ways.

A story that might illustrate this better than any is that of a young woman who was going off to college, only to find that her scholarships didn't quite cover the cost of living on campus. Her grandmother lived nearby, but the prospect of spending her undergraduate years in her grandmother's home was not the most appealing - this wasn't how she envisioned college, for sure! Having no alternative, though, she acquiesced and moved her stuff into the guest room in the back. It was difficult at first, for though she had always spent time with this grandmother growing up, she had never been particularly close to her. Unlike her other grandmother, who doted on her and did grandmotherly things like baking and crafts, this grandmother was more interested in friends, cards, and adult conversation.

Much to her surprise when, gradually over time, she began to understand where her grandmother had come from: a rural and very poor background during which her father died young, leaving her uneducated mother to raise five children on her own. She learned that her grandmother had to take work as a young woman, foregoing further education, to support herself, and fell in love with an older man - her grandfather - who had old-fashioned ideas about women working outside the house. Her grandmother, she came to discover, was a wicked smart and fun-loving person who had never been afforded the opportunities in life to develop all she could have been. Instead, she now spent her days tirelessly supporting her granddaughter's endeavors to achieve all that she had been denied.

It dawned on the granddaughter one day that her grandmother was no mere grandmother: she was a mentor, a protective mothering figure, and a best friend. That relationship impacted the way she would view relationships from there on, with empathy and joy in the discovery of connection where it didn't seem that one could exist. That was the Hygge spirit of the grandmother: she took pleasure in the small things in life, cooked with gusto, welcomed with open arms, and fostered love and happiness in all those she cared for. It would do us all good to take some time to foster those kinds of connections with our elders, if for nothing else than to teach us how to embrace Hygge practice in the face of anything the world throws at us.

Conclusion

If stress and anxiety haunt you, you must learn the "Hygge" method, the secret of happiness, thanks to which the Danes have been the happiest people in the world for over a hundred years.

When I first met the Hygge style, In a moment I went back with the memories and I lost myself for a few moments in the most intimate sensations related to my travels to Copenhagen and Oslo, thinking of how beautiful they are! When I returned home, full of nostalgia and good intentions to return to Denmark as soon as possible. I immediately started reading.

Page after page, with simple and soothing words, that book explained to me why the Danes are the happiest people in the world. Speaking of spaces full of familiar warmth and full of daily care, it teaches comfort as a personal compass to be reached through small rituals that have warmth at the center. That of a hot drink, that of a burning fireplace, of a soft and enveloping plaid.

The first place to look for Hygge, I began to understand, is home. Not a space where you can pass between a commitment and another, not a container, but a sweet concentrate of happiness and intimacy, an oasis where you can put love and attention because it belongs to us intimately. I am not talking about possession, but about belonging. I'm talking about getting in touch with yourself. A fulfilling environment for the soul as well as for the eyes, capable of transmitting ease through its colors, its shapes and its materials, capable of welcoming every time we return and welcoming us making us feel good. As if it were a smile, the idea is not to isolate oneself, but rather to surround oneself with family gestures to feel, always and everywhere, at home.

Going on with the reading, in fact, gradually I understood that every space that gives us these wonderful feelings of security and peace is Hygge. Because Hygge resembles an art, it is a lifestyle that welcomes your needs and supports them. I discovered and understood that the secret to simply being more satisfied is learning to enjoy true moments of full relaxation, and this is how every moment and every place that can protect and reassure me becomes happy. Hygge is also about spending and sharing time with those you love, for example sitting at the table with good friends enjoying the company without having to keep your guard up or (at least as far as I'm concerned) having my dog next to you.

Hygge is something intimate, there is no universal advice: everyone will be happy when they find their Hygge. I, looking inside myself, learned to find Hygge in my daily life. For me, for example, it means keeping my bookcase full of the books I love and then sitting down to read them and leaf through them on my plaid armchair, the same one where my grandmother once sat to rest. It is writing free thoughts on my thousand notebooks, looking at photos of my still child, taking care of my flowers, lighting my candles, preparing my cup of tea (which I have loved since I was a child).

From all this, the world remains outside because it is not hygging at all. Personally, in this lifestyle I have found my refuge from everything with which I sincerely find it increasingly difficult to deal with: individualism, widespread need to focus on having the illusion of being, be content with anything and anyone, with questionable and alienating places like, for example, panic Sundays in shopping centers. It is often right out there in that world that I experience the absolute sense of emptiness and loneliness. In all that fuss, in all those things of doubtful taste, in all those frightened people. Other effects only sadden me. That's why, instead, I choose to put love in my nest and, learning to look for my serenity there, I finally found it.

At the bottom I decided to make small changes at home, certain and sure that they would be worth more than any object I could buy, for example a garment to wear (often in reality without even needing it). A few touches were enough, which gave me a hand to make it warmer and more mine. A new color on the walls, soft cushions resting on the sofa, some wallpaper. When I don't prepare my trolley to go elsewhere, my home is now the place where I feel good. Sometimes it happens that you spend the whole weekend there. I welcome a few people, only the ones I feel comfortable with. I don't do anything special: often I don't even feel I need to watch a movie I like. I curl up in the little, simple things I love to do and that's enough for me to feel happy.

Finally, if you've found this book helpful in any way, an Amazon review is always welcome!